Table of Contents (cont.)

79. Use Words in Context 40
80. Test-Taking 40
81. Review Words and Their Definitions 41
82. Review Words and Their Definitions 41
83. Review Words and Their Definitions 42
84. Review Words and Their Definitions 42
85. Define Nouns 43
86. Classify Nouns 43
87. Use Nouns in Context/Write Headlines 44
88. Test-Taking 44
89. Define Verbs 45
90. Use Verbs in Context 45
91. Use the Past Tense of Verbs in Context 46
92. Test-Taking 46
93. Define Verbs 47
94. Add Suffixes to Change Verbs to Nouns 47
95. Use Words in Context 48
96. Test-Taking 48
97. Define Compound Words 49
98. Critical Thinking 49
99. Use Compound Words in Context 50
100. Test-Taking 50
101. Define Homophones 51
102. Use Homophones in Context 51
103. Write Rhymes 52
104. Test-Taking 52
105. Define Verbs 53
106. Determine Root Words/Define Words With
     Suffixes 53
107. Apply Vocabulary Words to Personal Life 54
108. Test-Taking 54
109. Review Words and Their Definitions 55
110. Review Words and Their Definitions 55
111. Review Words and Their Definitions 56
112. Review Words and Their Definitions 56
113. Define Verbs 57
114. Add Suffixes/Define Words With Suffixes 57
115. Use Words in Context/Write Hyperboles 58
116. Test-Taking 58
117. Define Easily Confused Words 59
118. Determine the Correct Word 59
119. Use Words in Context/Write Questions 60
120. Test-Taking 60
121. Define Nouns 61
122. Use Nouns in Context 61
123. Use Reference Sources 62

124. Test-Taking 62
125. Define Words With Prefixes and Suffixes 63
126. Use Words in Context 63
127. Apply Knowledge of Vocabulary Words to
     Everyday Life 64
128. Test-Taking 64
129. Define Homophones 65
130. Use Homophones in Context 65
131. Critical Thinking 66
132. Test-Taking 66
133. Define Compound Words 67
134. Use Compound Words in Context 67
135. Use Words in Context/Apply Personal
     Knowledge 68
136. Test-Taking 68
137. Review Words and Their Definitions 69
138. Review Words and Their Definitions 69
139. Review Words and Their Definitions 70
140. Review Words and Their Definitions 70
141. Define Words With Prefixes and Suffixes 71
142. Use Words in Context 71
143. Differentiate Between Nouns and Verbs 72
144. Test-Taking 72
145. Define Compound Words 73
146. Explore Alternate Meanings/Apply Personal
     Experience 73
147. Use Compound Words in Context/
     Write Headlines 74
148. Test-Taking 74
149. Define Number Words 75
150. Use Number Prefixes to Make New Words 75
151. Use Words With Number Prefixes in Context 76
152. Test-Taking 76
153. Identify Mythological/Legendary Creatures 77
154. Explore Mythological Words 77
155. Use Words in Context/Describe a Fantasy
     Experience 78
156. Test-Taking 78
157. Define Heteronyms 79
158. Define Heteronyms 79
159. Define Heteronyms 80
160. Determine Usage of Heteronyms 80
161. Use Words in Context/Write Question Sentences ..81
162. Test-Taking 81
Answer Keys 82

Introduction to the Teacher

Books in the *Daily Skill Builders: Vocabulary* series are designed to increase students' reading, writing, and speaking vocabulary by introducing new words, providing an opportunity for students to determine their meanings, and using the words in context. In addition, practice in standardized test-taking is emphasized.

Suggestions for Use

Each activity page is divided into two reproducible sections that can be cut apart and used separately. Activities could be used in class as a group or individually, or they can be assigned as homework. Transparencies of the activities can be made to help students participate as they follow along in class. Extra copies can be kept in your learning center for additional practice.

An alphabetical list of the vocabulary words introduced in this book is included on pages v–vi. Vocabulary words can be included in your weekly spelling list. Use the new words in context in class and encourage students to do so also. Being exposed to and using new words helps students develop a more extensive reading, writing, and speaking vocabulary.

Organization

Vocabulary words are introduced in groups of 10 to 12 words at a time. Four activities are included for each new group of words.

The first activity for each group of words involves defining the new words. Before students begin this activity, encourage them to read the words out loud together. At this age, many students have difficulty understanding the pronunciation guide in a dictionary. Saying the words helps them learn pronunciation. Students will need access to a good dictionary and a thesaurus. Include both a simple picture dictionary as well as one that is more advanced.

The second and third activities for each group offer variety to provide students with many different ways to approach learning vocabulary. They use words in context, write rhyming words and short poems, express opinions, and write sentences. Students learn synonyms and antonyms for words, differentiate between homophones, explore multiple meanings for the same word, write present and past tenses of verbs, use the singular and plural forms of nouns, and change adjectives to adverbs.

Since standardized testing is an important component of education, the fourth activity for each group provides practice in standardized test-taking formats. This helps students become familiar and comfortable with the format and provides test-taking practice.

The table of contents identifies the skills that students use to complete each activity. Review pages are included to reinforce what students have learned. An answer key is provided at the end of the book.

Both the No Child Left Behind Act and standardized testing require students to meet certain proficiency standards. The *Daily Skill Builders* in this book have been written with both of these sets of requirements in mind. Standards matrixes for selected states are provided on pages vii–ix. These give teachers the specific reading, writing, and language standards that are covered by each activity in this book. The National ELA Standards as supported by NCTE and IRA are listed on page x.

Vocabulary Words Used in This Book

absurd	barrier	command	detector	equip
accept	barter	commandment	device	equipment
accessories	basilisk	commercial	devise	estimate
accumulate	bicentennial	competent	dice	evaluate
accumulation	bilingual	complement	digest	evaluation
ace	biography	complex	dilate	exaggerate
achieve	blend	compliment	dimple	exaggeration
achievement	board	comprehend	direct	exceed
acquire	bored	comprehension	direction	except
admiration	bought	compromise	directive	exhaust
admire	bouillon	comrade	directly	experiment
advance	boulevard	condense	director	extend
advancement	boycott	conduct	directory	extension
advantage	brake	confine	disadvantage	extinguish
advice	break	confinement	dispenser	familiar
advise	bridal	conscious	display	fanfare
affect	bridle	consider	dissatisfied	fidget
aggravate	brought	considerable	doughboy	flagship
aid	brunch	consideration	downtrodden	flagstone
aide	buffet	contest	draft	focus
aisle	bullion	continual	dragnet	foreground
all together	burrow	continuous	drawback	forehand
aloof	campus	contradict	dreadful	foresight
altar	canapé	convey	dryad	forewarn
alter	cancel	cooperate	dual	foreword
alteration	cancellation	cooperation	duel	formal
alternate	canopy	cooperative	duplicate	fortnight
alternately	capable	counterclockwise	duplication	fourscore
alternative	capsule	culprit	duration	frail
altogether	carryover	deadline	dwindle	frantic
amaze	cater	debate	earthwork	freehand
amazement	census	decade	effect	freelance
ancestor	centaur	decathlon	emphasize	frontier
appliances	century	decline	employer	fugitive
appropriate	cereal	defiant	encourage	gatecrasher
arch	challenge	defy	encouragement	gracious
architect	chimera	deli	energetic	grandstand
ascent	choose	deliberate	enforce	grateful
assent	chose	dense	enforcement	gratuity
associate	cite	descendant	enlarge	greenhorn
attain	client	destination	enlargement	gumshoe
attorney	clinic	detach	enroll	harass
auction	clockwise	detachment	enrollment	harassment
autobiography	coast	detect	entertain	harpy
bandwagon	coastline	detection	entertainment	hasty
barnstorm	combine	detective	epidemic	haywire

v

Vocabulary Words Used in This Book (cont.)

hazard	loom	pasture	rebel	steeplejack
hermit	loose	patient	reconsider	stouthearted
hesitant	lopsided	peak	record	straight
hesitate	lose	peasants	redeem	strait
hesitation	lukewarm	pedal	reigns	substitute
highbrow	luxurious	peddle	reins	substitution
high-handed	magnificent	pentathlon	reinvest	subtle
hindsight	majority	perk	request	suburb
hoard	mansion	personnel	require	sufficient
horde	meander	pesticides	requirement	supervise
hostile	meddle	petty	reservation	supervision
hourglass	meek	phoenix	reserve	tableland
hover	mermaid	pique	residence	terminal
humerus	milestone	plain	residents	testify
humorous	millennium	plane	retire	textiles
ignite	mince	poor	retirement	thumbtack
illegible	minority	population	ripcord	tolerable
immense	minotaur	pore	safeguard	tremble
impound	misdirection	portrait	salon	tremendous
impractical	miser	postpone	sandhog	trendsetter
inappropriate	monotonous	pour	satisfied	tripod
incompetent	mural	practical	satyr	triumph
inconsiderate	mutter	prairie	schedule	turncoat
indifferent	naiad	pray	scrawny	unaltered
influence	negotiate	present	secure	unbearable
infomercial	negotiations	prey	serial	unconscious
informal	nonobservance	principal	sesquicentennial	uncooperative
intolerable	nook	principle	shorthand	undercoat
invest	nourish	produce	shorthanded	underhanded
investigate	nourishment	profit	showdown	undermine
investigation	nutritious	progress	shuffle	undertow
investigator	oasis	prohibit	siblings	undetectable
investor	object	prohibition	sideswipe	unfamiliar
irritate	observance	prophet	sight	unicycle
isle	observant	proposal	significant	unify
issue	observation	propose	simmer	vendor
jagged	observatory	proposition	site	versatile
jaywalk	observe	provocation	slouch	viewpoint
jitterbug	observer	provoke	spacious	volley
jubilant	occupation	pulley	spectator	workhorse
keepsake	occupy	pussyfoot	spendthrift	
ladyfinger	octave	quadruplets	sphinx	
layaway	openhanded	quartet	sprout	
legible	oppose	quench	standoff	
light-headed	opposition	quintet	startle	
limitation	oversight	range	stationary	
longhand	parasites	realtor	stationery	

vi

California Standards Matrix for Grades 5–6

LANGUAGE ARTS STANDARDS	ACTIVITIES
<u>READING</u>	
Identify and interpret figurative language and words with multiple meanings.	21, 23, 45, 46, 73, 74, 146, 157
Recognize the origins and meanings of frequently used foreign words in English, and use these words accurately in speaking and writing.	150, 151, 152
Understand and explain frequently used synonyms, antonyms, and homographs.	8, 14, 15, 16, 17, 20, 24, 34, 36, 64, 65, 70, 72, 77, 80, 92, 96, 100, 101, 104
Use word, sentence, and paragraph clues to determine meaning of unknown words.	1, 2, 4, 5, 7, 9, 10, 12, 13, 18, 25, 26, 27, 28, 29, 32, 33, 37, 38, 39, 40, 41, 42, 44, 45, 46, 48, 49, 50, 52, 53, 54, 55, 56, 57, 59, 60, 61, 62, 66, 67, 68, 69, 73, 75, 76, 78, 79, 81, 82, 83, 84, 85, 88, 89, 90, 93, 94, 95, 97, 102, 105, 106, 108, 109, 110, 111, 112, 113, 114, 115, 117, 118, 120, 121, 122, 123, 124, 125, 126, 128, 129, 130, 132, 133, 134, 136, 137, 138, 139, 140, 141, 142, 144, 145, 148, 149, 153, 154, 156, 158, 160
Analyze text that uses an organizational pattern (e.g., sequential or chronological order, compare and contrast).	42, 47
Make, modify, and confirm inferences, conclusions, or generalizations about text and support them with textual evidence and prior knowledge.	3, 11, 19, 22, 30, 51, 58, 59, 62, 98, 107, 127, 135, 146, 154
Distinguish facts, supported inferences, and opinions in text.	11, 63
<u>WRITING</u>	
Create well-developed, multiple-paragraph narrative and expository compositions.	71, 99, 131, 155
Use a variety of organizational patterns, including comparison and contrast; organization by categories; and arrangement by spatial order, order of importance, or climactic order.	42, 47, 99, 147, 155
<u>LANGUAGE CONVENTIONS</u>	
Use simple, compound, and compound-complex sentences; use effective coordination and subordination of ideas to express complete thoughts.	31, 71, 99, 115, 131, 147, 155
Identify and properly use indefinite pronouns and present perfect, past perfect, and future perfect verb tenses; ensure that verbs agree with compound subjects.	6, 7, 34, 87, 91, 94, 115, 131, 147, 155
Use correct capitalization.	31, 58, 66, 71, 91, 99, 103, 106, 119, 131, 155, 161
Spell roots, affixes, contractions, and syllable constructions correctly.	6, 7, 34, 71, 78, 91, 99, 106, 119, 131, 147, 155

Florida Standards Matrix for Grades 5–6

LANGUAGE ARTS STANDARDS	ACTIVITIES
READING	
Study word parts and meanings consistently across curricular content (e.g., affixes, multiple-meaning words, antonyms, synonyms, root words, homonyms, homophones).	4, 8, 9, 13, 14, 15, 16, 17, 18, 19, 20, 21, 23, 24, 34, 36, 40, 41, 44, 45, 46, 49, 52, 57, 60, 61, 64, 65, 70, 72, 73, 74, 77, 78, 80, 92, 96, 97, 100, 101, 104, 106, 114, 120, 126, 128, 129, 131, 132, 133, 136, 141, 143, 145, 149, 150, 151, 152, 157
Use resources (e.g., dictionary, thesaurus, encyclopedia, websites) to clarify word meanings.	1, 3, 5, 9, 13, 14, 17, 21, 29, 33, 37, 41, 43, 45, 46, 57, 58, 59, 78, 85, 114, 117, 123, 125, 129, 133, 141, 145, 146, 149, 150, 153, 154, 158
Use a variety of strategies to monitor texts (e.g., rereading, self-correcting, summarizing, checking other sources, using context and word structure clues).	2, 7, 10, 11, 12, 18, 19, 22, 23, 25, 26, 27, 28, 30, 32, 39, 45, 46, 48, 50, 51, 53, 54, 55, 56, 59, 60, 62, 67, 68, 69, 73, 79, 81, 82, 83, 84, 88, 89, 90, 93, 95, 102, 105, 108, 109, 110, 111, 112, 113, 116, 118, 121, 122, 124, 126, 127, 130, 134, 135, 137, 138, 139, 140, 142, 144, 146, 148, 149, 156, 160
Understand explicit and implicit ideas and information in texts (e.g., main idea, inferences, relevant supporting details, fact vs. opinion, generalizations, conclusions).	11, 63
Read and organize information from multiple sources for a variety of purposes (e.g., to support opinions, predictions, and conclusions; to write a research report; to conduct interviews).	43, 59, 146, 149
Analyze ways writers organize and present ideas (e.g., comparison–contrast, cause–effect, chronology).	42, 47
WRITING	
Use an effective organizational pattern and substantial support to achieve completeness.	99, 131, 155
Use devices to develop relationships among ideas (e.g., transitional devices, cause-and-effect relationships).	42, 47, 99, 155
Use a variety of sentence structures to reinforce ideas.	31, 71, 87, 99, 131, 147, 155, 161
Use conventions of punctuation and capitalization.	31, 58, 66, 71, 91, 99, 106, 107, 115, 119, 131, 147, 155
Use various parts of speech correctly in writing (e.g., subject-verb agreement, noun and verb forms, objective and subjective case pronouns, correct form of adjectives and adverbs).	1, 6, 7, 13, 15, 16, 31, 34, 39, 51, 58, 59, 62, 66, 71, 74, 75, 76, 87, 90, 91, 94, 99, 106, 107, 115, 119, 131, 134, 147, 155, 161
Use basic features of page format, including paragraph indentations and margins.	99, 131, 155
Write for a variety of occasions, audiences, and purposes.	31, 35, 37, 38, 51, 58, 59, 62, 66, 71, 87, 91, 98, 99, 103, 106, 107, 115, 119, 127, 131, 146, 147, 154, 155, 161
LANGUAGE	
Use appropriate words (e.g., figurative language, sensory words) to shape reactions, perceptions, and beliefs.	71, 87, 99, 115, 147, 155
Vary language according to situation, audience, and purpose.	71, 87, 99, 115, 131, 147, 155
Understand symbols, similes, metaphors, analogies, alliteration, and idiomatic language.	35, 115

Texas Standards Matrix for Grades 5–6

LANGUAGE ARTS STANDARDS	ACTIVITIES
READING	
Apply knowledge of letter-sound correspondences, structural analysis, and context to recognize words and identify root words with affixes.	2, 4, 5, 7, 8, 10, 12, 13, 14, 15, 16, 20, 24, 25, 26, 27, 28, 32, 34, 36, 39, 40, 41, 44, 45, 46, 48, 50, 52, 53, 54, 55, 56, 57, 58, 59, 60, 61, 62, 64, 65, 67, 68, 69, 70, 72, 73, 74, 75, 76, 77, 78, 79, 80, 81, 82, 83, 84, 85, 88, 89, 90, 92, 93, 95, 96, 97, 100, 101, 102, 104, 105, 108, 109, 110, 111, 112, 113, 114, 116, 118, 120, 121, 122, 124, 125, 126, 128, 129, 130, 132, 136, 137, 138, 139, 140, 141, 142, 144, 145, 148, 149, 151, 152, 156, 157
Locate the meanings, pronunciations, and derivations of unfamiliar words using a dictionary, a thesaurus, a glossary, and available technology.	1, 5, 9, 13, 14, 21, 29, 33, 37, 41, 43, 45, 46, 49, 57, 59, 61, 114, 117, 123, 125, 133, 149, 150, 153, 154, 158
Draw on experiences to bring meanings to words in context, such as multiple-meaning words.	3, 11, 19, 22, 23, 30, 38, 45, 46, 51, 58, 59, 127, 135, 146, 160
Follow strategies for comprehension while reading, such as rereading, using reference aids, searching for clues, and asking questions.	58, 59, 61, 154
Distinguish fact and opinion in various texts.	11, 63
Answer different types and levels of questions.	4, 8, 20, 32, 48, 52, 60, 64, 116, 136
LITERARY RESPONSE AND CONCEPTS	
Offer observations, make connections, react, speculate, interpret, and raise questions in response to texts.	11, 38, 51, 58, 59, 62, 66, 98, 107, 127
Interpret text ideas through journal writing, discussion, enactment, and media.	58, 155
Support responses by referring to relevant aspects of text and own experiences.	11, 51, 58, 59, 98, 107, 127
Analyze ways authors organize and present ideas, such as through cause/effect, compare/contrast, or chronologically.	42, 47
WRITING	
Write for a variety of audiences and purposes.	31, 35, 38, 51, 58, 59, 62, 66, 71, 78, 87, 91, 99, 103, 106, 107, 115, 119, 131, 146, 147, 155, 161
Compose original texts, applying the conventions of written language, such as capitalization, punctuation, and penmanship, to communicate clearly.	31, 35, 51, 58, 66, 71, 87, 91, 99, 106, 107, 115, 119, 131, 147, 155, 161
Write with accurate spelling of roots, inflections, affixes, and syllable constructions.	6, 7, 31, 34, 35, 51, 58, 59, 62, 66, 71, 78, 87, 91, 94, 99, 106, 107, 115, 119, 131, 147, 155
Use regular and irregular plurals correctly and adjust verbs for agreement.	62, 66, 71, 87, 91, 99, 115, 131, 134, 147, 155
Write in complete sentences, varying the types, such as compound and complex, to match meanings and purposes.	31, 35, 58, 66, 71, 78, 91, 99, 106, 107, 115, 119, 131, 155, 161
Use prepositional phrases, adjectives, and adverbs to make writing vivid and precise.	13, 15, 16, 58, 71, 87, 99, 115, 131, 155

National ELA Standards

(as supported by NCTE and IRA)

[reference: http://www.ncte.org/about/over/standards/110846.htm]

1. Students read a wide range of print and nonprint texts to build an understanding of texts, of themselves, and of the cultures of the United States and the world; to acquire new information; to respond to the needs and demands of society and the workplace; and for personal fulfillment. Among these texts are fiction and nonfiction, classic and contemporary works.

2. Students read a wide range of literature from many periods in many genres to build an understanding of the many dimensions (e.g., philosophical, ethical, aesthetic) of human experience.

3. Students apply a wide range of strategies to comprehend, interpret, evaluate, and appreciate texts. They draw on their prior experience, their interactions with other readers and writers, their knowledge of word meaning and of other texts, their word identification strategies, and their understanding of textual features (e.g., sound-letter correspondence, sentence structure, context, graphics).

4. Students adjust their use of spoken, written, and visual language (e.g., conventions, style, vocabulary) to communicate effectively with a variety of audiences and for different purposes.

5. Students employ a wide range of strategies as they write and use different writing process elements appropriately to communicate with different audiences for a variety of purposes.

6. Students apply knowledge of language structure, language conventions (e.g., spelling and punctuation), media techniques, figurative language, and genre to create, critique, and discuss print and nonprint texts.

7. Students conduct research on issues and interests by generating ideas and questions, and by posing problems. They gather, evaluate, and synthesize data from a variety of sources (e.g., print and nonprint texts, artifacts, people) to communicate their discoveries in ways that suit their purpose and audience.

8. Students use a variety of technological and information resources (e.g., libraries, databases, computer networks, video) to gather and synthesize information and to create and communicate knowledge.

9. Students develop an understanding of and respect for diversity in language use, patterns, and dialects across cultures, ethnic groups, geographic regions, and social roles.

10. Students whose first language is not English make use of their first language to develop competency in the English language arts and to develop understanding of content across the curriculum.

11. Students participate as knowledgeable, reflective, creative, and critical members of a variety of literacy communities.

12. Students use spoken, written, and visual language to accomplish their own purposes (e.g., for learning, enjoyment, persuasion, and the exchange of information).

ACTIVITY 1 · Define Nouns

Name: _____

Date: _____

Nouns name people, places, things, or ideas. All the nouns on this list name people.

Write the noun from the list that matches its definition. Use a dictionary if you are unsure of the meaning of a word.

ancestor	architect	attorney	client	comrade	culprit
descendant	miser	peasants	personnel	population	realtor

1. _____ a lawyer; one who practices law
2. _____ employees; workers
3. _____ a person guilty of a crime
4. _____ a close friend or companion
5. _____ number of people living in a certain area
6. _____ a person who designs buildings
7. _____ a relative who lived before you
8. _____ a person who shows buildings for rent or sale
9. _____ someone who goes to a professional for help; customer
10. _____ a relative who comes after you (children, grandchildren, etc.)
11. _____ one who doesn't want to spend any money, even if he has a lot; a tightwad; a cheapskate
12. _____ farmers and tenants who work for a monarch or other noble

ACTIVITY 2 · Use Nouns in Context

Name: _____

Date: _____

Write words from the list to complete the sentences.

ancestors	architect	attorney	clients	comrades	culprit
descendants	miser	peasants	personnel	population	realtor

1. _____ at the bakery take home leftovers at the end of the day.
2. Carla called a(n) _____ to help her write her will.
3. If the _____ opened his wallet, moths would probably fly out!
4. Many people claim to be _____ of Thomas Jefferson.
5. The _____ worked in the field from dawn to dusk.
6. The _____ was fined $1,000 for trespassing.
7. The Widget Company has many _____who buy from them regularly.
8. Tony and Michelle have been _____ since first grade.
9. What is the _____ of Monkey's Eyebrow, Kentucky?
10. From where did your _____ come originally?
11. Who was the _____ who designed the Taj Mahal in India?
12. Will you call a _____ to help you find a new apartment?

1

ACTIVITY 3 Apply Personal Knowledge to Everyday Life

Name: _____

Date: _____

1. Name two of your **ancestors**. _____ _____
2. Name two of your **comrades**. _____ _____
3. List three **descendants** of your grandparents other than yourself.

    _____ _____ _____

4. Frank Lloyd Wright was a famous **architect.** Look at photos of some of the buildings he designed. What do you think of his work? _____

    _____

5. Look in a telephone book. List two **realtors** in your city.

    _____ _____

6. Why would someone become a **client** of a realtor? _____

7. Look in a telephone book, and then list two **attorneys** in your city.

    _____ _____

8. List three cities. Use a reference source to find the **population** of these cities.

    _____ _____ _____

9. Name a book, story, or movie and the character who was a **culprit**.

    _____

ACTIVITY 4 Test-Taking

Name: _____

Date: _____

Circle "T" for true or "F" for false.

1. T F   A **miser** gives large amounts of money to charity.
2. T F   A **realtor** sells horses.
3. T F   An **architect** designs arches.
4. T F   An **attorney** would be the person to call if you wanted to rent an apartment.
5. T F   **Clients** are people who sell things to a company.
6. T F   **Comrades** are friends.
7. T F   A **culprit** is a person guilty of doing something wrong.
8. T F   **Peasants** were wealthy and lived in castles.
9. T F   **Personnel** are people employed by a company.
10. T F   The **population** of a city never changes.
11. T F   Your great-great-grandmother is an **ancestor** of yours.
12. T F   Your great-great-grandfather is a **descendant** of yours.

2

ACTIVITY 5 Define Verbs

Name: _____

Date: _____

Verbs are action words. Match the verbs with their definitions. Use a dictionary if you are unsure of the meaning of a word.

1. _____ attain
2. _____ barter
3. _____ decline
4. _____ mince
5. _____ mutter
6. _____ quench
7. _____ redeem
8. _____ testify
9. _____ tremble
10. _____ volley

a. to turn in (coupons, for example) and receive something in exchange

b. to refuse; to get sicker

c. to satisfy the need for something, especially drink

d. to give evidence, often in a courtroom

e. to shake, often due to fear

f. to speak softly so others cannot hear; to grumble

g. to trade one item or favor for another

h. to toss or hit something back and forth

i. to reach a goal

j. to cut or chop into very small pieces

ACTIVITY 6 Use the Past Tense of Verbs in Context

Name: _____

Date: _____

Past tense means that something happened before now. For most verbs, add *-ed* to form the past tense. When verbs end in *e*, drop the *e* and add *-ed*. If a verb ends in a consonant and *y*, change the *y* to *i* and add *-ed*. (Do not change the *y* to *i* if a vowel comes before the *y*.)

Write a sentence on another sheet of paper using the past tense of each verb. Use a dictionary if you are unsure of the meaning of a word.

1. attain
2. barter
3. decline
4. mince
5. mutter

6. quench
7. redeem
8. testify
9. tremble
10. volley

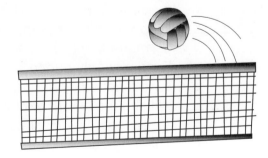

ACTIVITY 7 Use the Proper Tense of Verbs in Context

Name: _____

Date: _____

Use the present or past tense of the verbs on the list to complete the sentences.

attain	barter	decline	mince	mutter
quench	redeem	testify	tremble	volley

1. Before people had money, they used the _____ system to exchange goods and services.
2. Dennis and Denise _____ the ball back and forth before the tennis match.
3. Do you like to be around people who _____ and complain a lot?
4. Jeremy was pleased when he _____ his goal of losing ten pounds.
5. I offered Shelby a ride, but she _____ because it was a great day for a walk.
6. It's going to take a large drink of water to _____ my thirst after the ballgame.
7. Rachel _____ in court about what she saw on April 1.
8. The frightened mouse _____ when it saw the cat.
9. This recipe calls for _____ sardines and a chopped rutabaga.
10. You can _____ your tokens for free gifts at the back counter.

ACTIVITY 8 Test-Taking

Name: _____

Date: _____

Write the letter of the answer that would best replace the boldface word(s).

1. _____ Marcus **reached** his goal when he saved $100.
   a. attain   b. attained   c. obtain   d. obtained
2. _____ Tom **traded** two old baseball mitts for a new one.
   a. bartered   b. barter   c. will buy   d. bought
3. _____ Grandpa's health **went downhill** after he broke his hip.
   a. declined   b. reclined   c. decline   d. inclined
4. _____ If you **chop up** onions and fry them, they add flavor to hotdogs.
   a. slice   b. minced   c. cook   d. mince
5. _____ Who will help me plant the wheat? "Not I," the goose **said in a low voice**.
   a. mutter   b. shouted   c. muttered   d. yelled
6. _____ Even a twenty-ounce soda did not **satisfy** his thirst.
   a. quenched   b. quench   c. replace   d. make happy
7. _____ Will the restaurant **exchange** that coupon if it is out of date?
   a. accept   b. reject   c. redeem   d. redeemed
8. _____ The judge asked Brandon **to tell the truth** about what he saw.
   a. testified   b. swear   c. promise   d. testify
9. _____ The thought of jumping out of an airplane with a parachute made Gina **shake**.
   a. fearful   b. tremble   c. relax   d. scared

ACTIVITY 9 Define Compound Words   Name:_____

Date:_____

A **compound word** combines two or more words to make a new word that expresses a single idea. *Firefly*, *warthog*, and *foxhole* are compound words. Sometimes the meaning of the new word isn't clear, even though you know the meaning of both words used.

Draw a line to separate the compound words into single words. Use a dictionary to write a brief definition for each word.

1. bandwagon_____
2. clockwise _____
3. counterclockwise_____
4. deadline _____
5. foreword _____
6. fourscore _____
7. grandstand _____
8. greenhorn _____
9. hourglass _____
10. steeplejack _____

ACTIVITY 10 Use Compound Words in Context   Name:_____

Date:_____

Write words from the list to complete the sentences.

| bandwagon | counterclockwise | deadline | foreword | fourscore |
| grandstand | greenhorn | hourglass | steeplejacks | |

1. _____ build and do maintenance on tall structures, such as church steeples.
2. Before people had clocks, they used a(n) _____ to measure time.
3. If you read the _____, you will understand the novel better.
4. If you spin _____ for too long, you will get just as dizzy as when you spin clockwise.
5. Phil usually made a fool of himself when he began to _____ to impress his friends.
6. The author had to complete the novel by April 1 to meet her _____.
7. The first words of Abraham Lincoln's Gettysburg Address are "_____ and seven years ago..."
8. When an easterner traveled to the Old West, he was often called a _____ because he didn't know much about how to survive there.
9. When her friends all began working at the animal shelter center, Holly jumped on the _____ too, even though she had no interest in animals.

ACTIVITY 11 Use Compound Words in Context/Write Opinions

Name:_____

Date:_____

Answer the following questions on another sheet of paper.

1. Would you like to work as a steeplejack? Why or why not?
2. How do you feel when you must complete something by a deadline?
3. Why would it be difficult to tell the exact time using an hourglass?
4. Do you usually read the foreword of a book? Why or why not?
5. What is your opinion of people who grandstand?
6. Would you rather jog clockwise or counterclockwise around a track? Why?
7. How old will you be fourscore years from now?
8. What would you like to learn how to do, even though you would be a greenhorn at first?
9. The phrase "to jump on the bandwagon" means to support a popular cause or fad. If all of your friends "jumped on the bandwagon" by wearing something that was the latest fad, would you do it too, even if you didn't like it? Why or why not?

ACTIVITY 12 Test-Taking

Name:_____

Date:_____

Circle "T" for true or "F" for false.

1. T F A **deadline** is a line that has died.
2. T F A **foreword** means the first four words of a document.
3. T F An **hourglass** is a large glass of soda that takes about an hour to drink.
4. T F Being a **steeplejack** is a good job for someone afraid of heights.
5. T F **Clockwise** means a smart clock—one that does not let you oversleep.
6. T F **Fourscore** means 80.
7. T F If you walk **counterclockwise**, you go around in a circle to the left.
8. T F In a parade, a band rides on the **bandwagon**.
9. T F Some lizards have **greenhorns**.
10. T F To **grandstand** means to show off.

Gettysburg Address

Fourscore and seven years ago…

ACTIVITY 13 Define Adjectives

Name:_____

Date:_____

Adjectives are words that describe nouns.

Example: We bounced down the *bumpy gravel* road in a *rickety old pickup* truck. *Bumpy* and *gravel* describe the road. *Rickety, old,* and *pickup* describe the truck.

All words on this list are adjectives. Write the adjective from the list to match its definition. Use a dictionary if you are unsure of the meaning of a word.

absurd	aloof	dense	dreadful	energetic	familiar
frail	gracious	grateful	jagged	luxurious	

1. cold and unfriendly _____
2. well-known _____
3. very fancy; elegant; plush _____
4. uneven _____
5. thick _____
6. thankful _____
7. terrible _____
8. ridiculous and unbelievable; silly _____
9. polite; kind _____
10. lively; filled with energy _____
11. in poor health; weak _____

ACTIVITY 14 Write Antonyms and Synonyms for Adjectives

Name:_____

Date:_____

An **antonym** is a word that means the opposite. A **synonym** is a word that means nearly the same as another word.

Write an antonym and a synonym for each word. Use a dictionary if you are unsure of the meaning of a word.

	Antonyms	**Synonyms**
1. absurd	_____	_____
2. aloof	_____	_____
3. dense	_____	_____
4. dreadful	_____	_____
5. energetic	_____	_____
6. familiar	_____	_____
7. frail	_____	_____
8. gracious	_____	_____
9. grateful	_____	_____
10. jagged	_____	_____
11. luxurious	_____	_____
12. tremendous	_____	_____

ACTIVITY 15 Use Adjectives in Context   Name:_____

Date:_____

Write words from the list to replace the boldface words.

aloof	dense	dreadful	energetic	familiar
frail	gracious	grateful	jagged	tremendous

1. When Terry caught a **terrible** cold, she felt miserable. _____
2. We watched the **lively** squirrel hide acorns in the garden. _____
3. When she saw her grandmother after being away for a year, Sara realized how **weak** her grandmother had become. _____
4. The survivors made their way through the **thick**, steamy jungle. _____
5. They couldn't find any **known** landmarks to guide them back to base. _____
6. From the top of the cliff, we looked down on a jumble of **sharp, uneven** rocks. _____
7. Cats can be very **cold and distant** when they want to be. _____
8. We were **thankful** for the opportunity. _____
9. Our **polite and kind** hostess made us feel right at home. _____
10. Our trip was a **terrific** experience. _____

ACTIVITY 16 Test-Taking   Name:_____

Date:_____

Write "A" if the words are antonyms. Write "S" if they are synonyms.

1. _____ absurd and ridiculous
2. _____ dense and thick
3. _____ friendly and aloof
4. _____ great and tremendous
5. _____ kind and gracious
6. _____ luxurious and elegant
7. _____ shoddy and luxurious
8. _____ strong and frail
9. _____ terrific and dreadful
10. _____ thankless and grateful
11. _____ tired and energetic
12. _____ weak and frail

13. _____ aloof and distant
14. _____ familiar and known
15. _____ gracious and unkind
16. _____ jagged and broken
17. _____ lively and energetic
18. _____ reasonable and absurd
19. _____ smooth and jagged
20. _____ terrible and dreadful
21. _____ thankful and grateful
22. _____ thin and dense
23. _____ unknown and familiar
24. _____ wonderful and tremendous

ACTIVITY 17   Define Homophones

Name:_____

Date:_____

Homophones are words that are pronounced the same but are spelled differently and have different meanings.

Write the homophone from the list to match its meaning. Use a dictionary if you are unsure of the meaning of a word. Not all of the words will be used.

aid	aide	aisle	altar	alter	bridal	bridle	cereal
dual	duel	hoard	horde	isle	plain	plane	poor
pour	pray	prey	profit	prophet	serial	sight	site

1. _____ walkway
2. _____ victim
3. _____ seer
4. _____ earnings
5. _____ a contest
6. _____ angry mob
7. _____ help
8. _____ to change
9. _____ double
10. _____ simple
11. _____ horse's harness
12. _____ breakfast grain

13. _____ flat surface
14. _____ without money
15. _____ a place
16. _____ save
17. _____ rain heavily
18. _____ helper

ACTIVITY 18   Determine Correct Homophones

Name:_____

Date:_____

Circle the correct word from each pair of homophones.

1. Misers are people who (hoard / horde) their money.
2. Put the (bridal / bridle) on your horse, and I'll take you to see a terrific (cite / site / sight).
3. Can you (cite / sight / site) the address of your favorite Internet (cite / sight / site)?
4. Cats often (pray / prey) on mice, but mine just likes to sit on the windowsill.
5. Do you enjoy watching (cereal / serial) movies?
6. Mr. Johnson hired Charles as his (aid / aide).
7. The (bridal / bridle) party walked slowly down the (aisle / isle) to the (altar / alter).
8. The gingham dog and the calico cat fought a (dual / duel).
9. The (poor / pore / pour) woman's hands shook so much she couldn't (poor / pore / pour) the water.
10. The (profit / prophet) made no (profit / prophet) from his predictions.
11. What kind of (cereal / serial) would you like for breakfast today?

ACTIVITY 19 Use Homophones in Context/
Relate Words to Everyday Life

Name:_____

Date:_____

Write an example for each item.

1. A gorgeous sight _____
2. A person who might employ an aide _____
3. A place that is an isle _____
4. A prophet _____
5. A story, book, or movie that is part of a serial _____
6. An animal and its prey _____
7. A place with an aisle _____
8. Any type of animal found in a large horde _____
9. Something people do for profit _____
10. Something people may hoard _____
11. Something that can aid you when you study _____
12. Something you can alter _____
13. Something that is plain _____
14. Something you can pour _____
15. Your favorite type of cereal _____

ACTIVITY 20 Test-Taking

Name:_____

Date:_____

Write the letter of the answer that best matches the meaning of the word.

1. _____ aid   a. help   b. aide   c. fix   d. helper
2. _____ alter   a. table   b. altar   c. move   d. change
3. _____ aisle   a. walkway   b. island   c. isle   d. church
4. _____ bridle   a. wedding   b. bride   c. harness   d. horse
5. _____ cereal   a. series   b. serial   c. toast   d. breakfast food
6. _____ cite   a. quote   b. place   c. view   d. Internet
7. _____ dual   a. contest   b. two   c. lots   d. one
8. _____ aide   a. help   b. helper   c. companion   d. friend
9. _____ pour   a. not rich   b. drink   c. faucet   d. rain heavily
10. _____ prey   a. request   b. victim   c. mouse   d. cat
11. _____ duel   a. two   b. dice   c. contest   d. game
12. _____ hoard   a. group   b. flock   c. crowd   d. collect
13. _____ horde   a. crowd   b. save   c. collect   d. reach
14. _____ isle   a. walkway   b. island   c. Alcatraz   d. Cuba
15. _____ plain   a. fancy   b. airplane c. simple   d. level
16. _____ site   a. Internet   b. place   c. view   d. quote

10

ACTIVITY 21 Define Words With Multiple Meanings

Name:_____

Date:_____

Some words can be used in more than one way and have different meanings. Write your answers on another sheet of paper. Use a dictionary if you are unsure of the meaning of a word.

1. An **associate** is a person with whom you spend time, such as a classmate or co-worker. What does it mean *to associate* with someone?
2. A **challenge** is a difficult task. What does *to challenge* mean?
3. A **compromise** is an agreement between two people or groups. Each person may need to give in a little bit to make it work. What does it mean *to compromise*?
4. **To display** means to show. What is a *display*?
5. **To estimate** means to make a guess based on facts. What does *estimate* mean when it is used as a noun?
6. An **experiment** is a test or a trial. What does *experiment* mean when it is used as a verb?
7. A **patient** is a person under a doctor's care. What does it mean *to be patient*?
8. A **schedule** is a timetable or listing of when events will take place. What does it mean *to schedule* an appointment?
9. **To influence** means to affect a decision. What does *influence* mean when it is used as a noun?
10. **Secure** means safe. What does *secure* mean when it is used as a verb?

ACTIVITY 22 Use Words With Multiple Meanings in Context/Relate Words to Personal Life

Name:_____

Date:_____

Answer the following questions on another sheet of paper.

1. With whom do you most like to associate?
2. Describe a challenge you have faced recently.
3. Describe a time when you've made a compromise with someone.
4. What type of museum display do you most enjoy?
5. Describe a situation where making an estimate is a good idea.
6. Describe an experiment you would like to do.
7. Who has the most influence on you?
8. Whom do you influence?
9. Describe a time when it was difficult for you to be patient.
10. What is on your schedule for the rest of today?
11. Describe a place where you feel secure.

ACTIVITY 23 Use Words With Multiple Meanings in Context

Name:_____

Date:_____

Write singular or plural words from the list to complete the sentences.

associate	challenge	compromise	display	estimate
experiment	influence	patient	schedule	secure

1. Do you allow TV commercials to _____ what you buy?
2. Do you have room in your busy _____ to meet me for lunch?
3. Doris made sure all the doors and windows were _____ before she went to bed.
4. How many geese would you _____ are in the marsh?
5. I _____ you to get an *A* on your next math test.
6. If you and your sister can't _____ on where to go today, we'll stay home.
7. I'll _____ the chart on the overhead so everyone can see it.
8. It's difficult to be a new _____ when you don't know all the other employees.
9. My Aunt Luvina often _____ with new recipes when she cooks.
10. Several of Dr. Brown's _____ cancelled their appointments due to the snowstorm.

ACTIVITY 24 Test-Taking

Name:_____

Date:_____

Write the letter of the answer that is not a definition for the word.

1. _____ associate   a. co-worker   b. boss
   c. someone with whom you spend time   d. classmate
2. _____ challenge   a. dare   b. to test   c. accept   d. to confront
3. _____ compromise   a. cooperate   b. promise   c. give and take   d. agree
4. _____ display   a. hide   b. to show   c. an exhibit   d. reveal
5. _____ estimate   a. guess   b. approximate   c. exact amount   d. about
6. _____ experiment   a. test   b. to try   c. certain   d. attempt
7. _____ influence   a. affect   b. sway   c. persuade   d. disagree
8. _____ patient   a. wrong   b. calm   c. serene   d. sick person
9. _____ secure   a. safe   b. hazard   c. protected   d. locked
10. _____ schedule   a. make an appointment   b. timetable
    c. an appointment   d. listing of events

ACTIVITY 25   Review Words and Their Definitions

Name:_____

Date:_____

Match the words with their definitions.

1. _____ architect	a. dare
2. _____ attorney	b. to toss or hit something back and forth
3. _____ challenge	c. someone who goes to a professional for help; customer
4. _____ client	d. guess
5. _____ compromise	e. cooperate
6. _____ comrade	f. affect
7. _____ culprit	g. person who shows buildings for rent or sale
8. _____ estimate	h. farmers and tenants who work for a monarch or other noble
9. _____ experiment	i. a lawyer; one who practices law
10. _____ influence	j. to try
11. _____ patient	k. a close friend or companion
12. _____ peasant	l. a person who designs buildings
13. _____ personnel	m. calm
14. _____ realtor	n. employees; workers
15. _____ volley	o. a person guilty of a crime

ACTIVITY 26   Review Words and Their Definitions

Name:_____

Date:_____

Match the words with their definitions.

1. _____ absurd	a. very fancy; elegant; plush
2. _____ aloof	b. cold and unfriendly
3. _____ attain	c. to satisfy the need for something, especially drink
4. _____ dense	d. to give evidence, often in a courtroom
5. _____ dreadful	e. to shake, often due to fear
6. _____ familiar	f. to speak softly so others cannot hear; to grumble
7. _____ frail	g. to reach a goal
8. _____ gracious	h. ridiculous and unbelievable
9. _____ jagged	i. uneven
10. _____ luxurious	j. wonderful; great
11. _____ mutter	k. terrible
12. _____ quench	l. well-known
13. _____ testify	m. in poor health; weak
14. _____ tremble	n. polite; kind
15. _____ tremendous	o. thick

13

ACTIVITY 27 Review Words and Their Definitions

Name: _____

Date: _____

Match the words with their definitions.

1. _____ aid	a. grains, usually eaten for breakfast
2. _____ aide	b. a table in a church
3. _____ aisle	c. a harness for a horse
4 . _____ altar	d. simple; unadorned
5. _____ alter	e. a walkway
6. _____ bridal	f. an island
7. _____ bridle	g. helper
8. _____ cereal	h. having to do with a bride
9. _____ cite	i. to collect; to save
10. _____ dual	j. to quote
11. _____ duel	k. to change
12. _____ hoard	l. to help
13. _____ horde	m. an angry mob
14. _____ isle	n. double
15. _____ plain	o. a contest

ACTIVITY 28 Review Words and Their Definitions

Name: _____

Date: _____

Match the words with their definitions.

1. _____ bandwagon	a. in a circle from left to right
2. _____ clockwise	b. eighty
3. _____ counterclockwise	c. a novice; beginner
4. _____ deadline	d. act up; show off
5. _____ foreword	e. to rain heavily
6. _____ fourscore	f. in a circle from right to left
7. _____ grandstand	g. calm
8. _____ greenhorn	h. a simple device with sand for telling time
9. _____ hourglass	i. a popular cause; a fad
10. _____ mince	j. an introduction to a book, story, or movie
11. _____ patient	k. to cut or chop into very small pieces
12. _____ pour	l. victim
13. _____ pray	m. a timetable
14. _____ prey	n. time limit
15. _____ schedule	o. to request

ACTIVITY 29 Define Nouns

Name:_____

Date:_____

Nouns are words that name people, places, things, or ideas. All the nouns on this list name things. Match the nouns with their definitions. Use a dictionary if you are unsure of the meaning of a word.

_____ 1. boulevard   a. a place that sells cooked or prepared foods

_____ 2. burrow   b. an area where cattle, sheep, or other domestic animals graze

_____ 3. campus   c. an area of flat grassland with few trees

_____ 4. clinic   d. the place to which a person or object is going

_____ 5. coastline   e. a small alcove

_____ 6. deli   f. an underground home for an animal

_____ 7. destination   g. the buildings and grounds of a school

_____ 8. frontier   h. a place in the desert where there is water

_____ 9. nook   i. a region beyond a settled area

_____ 10. oasis   j. a place that provides medical help

_____ 11. pasture   k. the area where land meets a body of water

_____ 12. prairie   l. a wide street with trees along the sides

---

ACTIVITY 30 Relate Vocabulary Words to Everyday Life

Name:_____

Date:_____

Use a reference source if you need help with the answers.
1. Name a boulevard in your city. _____
2. Name an animal that lives in a burrow. _____
3. Name a campus in your city or state. _____
4. Name a clinic in your area. _____
5. Where is the nearest coastline? _____
6. What do you like to get from a deli? _____
7. If you could go anywhere, what destination would you choose? _____
   Why? _____
8. At one time, Pennsylvania was the western frontier. Where could you find a frontier today?

   _____
9. If you had a comfy chair in a small nook, what would you do there? _____

   _____
10. Besides water, what would you find in an oasis? _____
11. What kinds of animals graze in a pasture? _____
12. What kinds of plants grow on a prairie? _____

ACTIVITY 31 Use Nouns in Context/ Write Questions

Name: _____

Date: _____

Use each word in a question sentence. Be certain to punctuate correctly.

1. boulevard _____

_____

2. burrow _____

_____

3. campus _____

_____

4. clinic _____

_____

5. coastline _____

_____

6. deli _____

_____

7. destination _____

_____

ACTIVITY 32 Test-Taking

Name: _____

Date: _____

Circle "T" for true or "F" for false.

1. T F   A **deli** is a great place to buy sandwiches and salads.

2. T F   A **destination** is where you end up when you get lost.

3. T F   A **nook** is a small hook for hanging hats and umbrellas.

4. T F   A **prairie** is usually a very hilly area.

5. T F   All **coastlines** are sandy beaches.

6. T F   **Boulevard** means exactly the same as street.

7. T F   Many people live in **burrows**.

8. T F   Nothing grows in a **pasture**. It is like a desert.

9. T F   People go to a **clinic** when they are sick.

10. T F   Students attend classes on a **campus**.

11. T F   There are no more **frontiers** on Earth.

12. T F   You could find an **oasis** in the middle of a large prairie.

ACTIVITY 33 Define Verbs

Name: _____

Date: _____

Write the verb from the list to match its definition. Use a dictionary if you are unsure of the meaning of a word.

| contradict | defy | dwindle | exceed | extinguish |
| ignite | slouch | startle | triumph | unify |

1. _____ to do something you were told not to do; challenge; dare
2. _____ to go beyond the limits; take more than you should
3. _____ to cause something to catch fire
4. _____ to put out a fire
5. _____ to say the opposite of what someone else says; oppose
6. _____ to sit or stand with poor posture; slump
7. _____ to slowly decrease or run out
8. _____ to surprise, frighten, or alarm someone
9. _____ to unite, join, or bring together
10. _____ to win a victory or overcome an obstacle

ACTIVITY 34 Find Antonyms for Verbs

Name: _____

Date: _____

Write the present or past tense of the verbs from the list that are the antonyms of the bold words. Use a dictionary if you are unsure of the meaning of a word.

| acquire | contradict | defy | dwindle | exceed | extinguish |
| ignite | postpone | slouch | startle | triumph | unify |

1. The principal hoped to **divide** the student body at the rally. _____
2. When Leon won the race, it was the greatest **loss** in his life. _____
3. If you **comply** with a police officer's orders, you will get into trouble. _____
4. It took us an hour to **extinguish** the grill to cook the hamburgers. _____
5. Never **do now** until tomorrow what you can do today. _____
6. Please **light** your campfire before going for a hike. _____
7. Robert Browning wrote, "Ah, but a man's reach should **underachieve** his grasp. Or what's a Heaven for?" _____
8. The loud thunder **calmed** Carrie. _____
9. The pile of dirty clothes **got bigger** as we did the laundry. _____
10. Do you plan to **give away** a new computer? _____
11. Troy always **sat up straight**. _____
12. Fred didn't have many friends because he always **agreed with** others. _____

ACTIVITY 35 Write Alliterative Sentences

Name: _____

Date: _____

Alliteration is the use of several words together that begin with the same sound.

Example: Anna acquired eight acorns for Andrew.

For each word, write a short alliterative sentence on another sheet of paper. Use at least three words that begin with the same letter as the verb listed.

1. acquire
2. contradict
3. defy
4. exceed
5. extinguish

6. ignite
7. postpone
8. slouch
9. startle
10. triumph

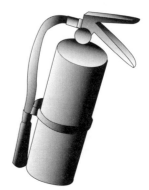

ACTIVITY 36 Test-Taking

Name: _____

Date: _____

Write the letter of the answer that best matches the definition.

1. _____ to obtain   a. lose   b. reach   c. acquire   d. misplace
2. _____ to say the opposite a. talk   b. reply   c. agree   d. contradict
3. _____ to challenge   a. stop   b. defy   c. agree   d. prevent
4. _____ to slowly decrease   a. descend   b. dwindle   c. increase   d. fall down
5. _____ to go beyond a limit a. exceed   b. decrease   c. recess   d. watch
6. _____ to put out a fire   a. ignite   b. water   c. reset   d. extinguish
7. _____ to start a fire   a. extinguish b. matches   c. ignite   d. charcoal
8. _____ to delay   a. stop   b. slouch   c. postpone   d. begin
9. _____ poor posture   a. slouch   b. reach   c. backache   d. sit
10. _____ to surprise or alarm a. unify   b. startle   c. shock   d. fire
11. _____ to win a victory   a. postpone   b. defy   c. triumph   d. lose
12. _____ to unite   a. agree   b. one item   c. tie   d. unify

18

ACTIVITY 37 Define Adjectives

Name:_____

Date:_____

Adjectives are words that describe nouns. All the words on this list are adjectives.

Write a short definition for each adjective. Use a dictionary if you are unsure of the meaning of a word.

1. frantic _____
2. immense _____
3. magnificent _____
4. monotonous _____
5. nutritious _____
6. petty _____
7. scrawny _____
8. significant _____
9. spacious _____
10. subtle _____
11. sufficient _____
12. versatile _____

ACTIVITY 38 Relate Vocabulary Words to Everyday Life

Name:_____

Date:_____

Write an example for each item.

1. the amount of soda you consider **sufficient** for one day

_____

2. an object that is **immense** _____

3. a view that is **magnificent** _____

4. something you find **monotonous** _____

5. food that is **nutritious** _____

6. something **petty** that annoys you _____

7. a time when you were **subtle** _____

8. something that makes people feel **frantic** _____

9. a time when someone showed that he or she was **versatile**

_____

ACTIVITY 39 Use Adjectives in Context

Name:_____

Date:_____

Write adjectives from the list to complete the sentences.

> frantic   magnificent   nutritious   petty   scrawny
> significant   spacious   sufficient   versatile

1. Don't let the _____ things bug you. They aren't worth it.
2. Fruits and vegetables are very _____ snacks.
3. Hal's room was so messy he knew it would take a _____ amount of work to get it clean.
4. I think three cookies are _____ for now, or you will spoil your appetite for supper.
5. People often feel _____ when they are running late.
6. The baby bird was so _____ you could see its bones when it shivered.
7. The Grand Canyon is a _____ sight!
8. The musician was so _____, he could play seven different instruments at the same time.
9. The song "America, the Beautiful," written by Katharine Lee Bates, begins with the words: "Oh beautiful, for _____ skies, for amber waves of grain."

ACTIVITY 40 Test-Taking

Name:_____

Date:_____

Circle "T" for true or "F" for false.

1. T   F   A **magnificent** sight is one that is wonderful.
2. T   F   A **petty** event is very pretty.
3. T   F   An animal that does not get enough to eat would become **scrawny**.
4. T   F   **Monotonous** tasks help people stay alert.
5. T   F   **Nutritious** foods should be avoided.
6. T   F   Someone who is **versatile** only knows how to do one thing.
7. T   F   Something **immense** is very large.
8. T   F   **Spacious** means lovely blue skies.
9. T   F   **Sufficient** means much more than is needed.
10. T   F   The birth of a child is a **significant** event in a family.
11. T   F   To be **subtle** means to be very obvious.
12. T   F   When people are **frantic**, they are calm.

ACTIVITY 41 Define Compound Words

Name: _____

Date: _____

A **compound word** combines two or more words to make a new word that expresses a single idea. *Bandwagon*, *greenhorn*, and *steeplejack* are compound words. Sometimes the meaning of the new word isn't clear, even though you know the meaning of both words used.

Draw a line to separate the compound words into single words. Use a dictionary to write a brief definition for each word.

1. drawback _____
2. layaway _____
3. viewpoint _____
4. gumshoe _____
5. ripcord _____
6. showdown _____
7. sideswipe _____
8. spendthrift _____
9. trendsetter _____
10. turncoat _____
11. What is one drawback of being a teenager? _____
_____

ACTIVITY 42 Use Compound Words in Context/Write Causes and Effects

Name: _____

Date: _____

Finish each sentence by writing a cause. Use another sheet of paper if you need more room.

1. Allen thought being short was a drawback because _____.
2. Because _____, Ben became a turncoat.
3. Molly called the gumshoe for help because _____.
4. Because _____, she couldn't put any items on layaway.
5. He knew there would soon be a showdown with his brother because _____.

Finish each sentence by writing an effect.

6. Because he could see her viewpoint, he _____.
7. Because the ripcord didn't work, _____.
8. Because he was such a spendthrift, _____.
9. Many people _____
_____ because the model was a trendsetter.

ACTIVITY 43   Write Compound Words

Name:_____

Date:_____

Use any reference source if you need help with this activity.

1. Write five compound words that include the word back. (*Example:* backtrack)

   _____ _____ _____ _____ _____

2. Write five compound that are animal names. (*Example:* seahorse)

   _____ _____ _____ _____ _____

3. Write five compound words that are plants. (*Example:* grapevine)

   _____ _____ _____ _____ _____

4. Write five compound words that are place names. (*Example:* Greenbush)

   _____ _____ _____ _____ _____

5. Write five compound words that are people's names. (*Example:* Rosemary)

   _____ _____ _____ _____ _____

6. Write five compound words that are in your classroom. (*Example:* textbook)

   _____ _____ _____ _____ _____

ACTIVITY 44   Test-Taking

Name:_____

Date:_____

Circle "T" for true or "F" for false.

1.   T   F   A **ripcord** is an important part of a parachute.
2.   T   F   To **layaway** means to sleep late.
3.   T   F   A **gumshoe** is a person who works for a bubblegum factory.
4.   T   F   A **trendsetter** is one who is a leader in what will become popular.
5.   T   F   A **showdown** is a disagreement between two people or groups.
6.   T   F   To **sideswipe** something means to put your credit card through the ATM machine.
7.   T   F   A **spendthrift** is a compulsive shopper.
8.   T   F   A **turncoat** is a person who wears her clothes inside out.
9.   T   F   A person's **viewpoint** is his outlook on a situation.
10. T   F   A **drawback** is what you do when you are ready to shoot an arrow from a bow.

ACTIVITY 45 Define Words With Multiple Meanings

Name:_____

Date:_____

The words on this list have several different meanings and can be used as more than one part of speech. Write words from the list next to their definitions. Words can be used more than once. Use a dictionary if you are unsure of the meaning of a word.

coast   complex   debate   dice   issue

1. _____ a formal argument
2. _____ a matter of concern
3. _____ an area with many apartments or offices located together
4. _____ something produced, published, or offered, such as special stamps or a copy of a magazine
5. _____ the area where land meets a large body of water
6. _____ to argue
7. _____ to chop into small pieces
8. _____ to produce something for distribution
9. _____ to glide down an incline without effort
10. _____ two or more game cubes

ACTIVITY 46 Define Words With Multiple Meanings

Name:_____

Date:_____

The words on this list have several different meanings and can be used as more than one part of speech. Write words from the list next to their definitions. Words can be used more than once. Use a dictionary if you are unsure of the meaning of a word.

commercial   digest   draft   exhaust   focus

1. _____ a cold breeze felt inside a building
2. _____ a collection of previously published articles, essays, or reports
3. _____ an advertisement
4. _____ to use up all of something
5. _____ to select from a group for military service
6. _____ moneymaking
7. _____ the center or point of concentration
8. _____ to absorb or understand something
9. _____ to concentrate on something
10. _____ to select from a group for a sports team
11. _____ fumes from an engine
12. _____ to take in food and convert it to energy

ACTIVITY 47 Use Words in Context/ Write Causes and Effects

Name: _____

Date: _____

Finish the sentences by writing a cause or effect. Use another sheet of paper for your answers.

1. _____, because he was coasting down a hill on his bike.
2. The problem was very complex, so Jon _____.
3. We sailed along the coast because _____.
4. _____ because there was a draft in the hall.
5. Wendy and Will held a debate on the issue because _____.
6. Barry shook a pair of sixes with his dice ten times in a row, so _____.
7. _____, so the professor bought a copy of the historical digest.
8. Because of the storm, Jenna could not focus on _____.
9. _____ caused Polly to exhaust all her energy.
10. Although he was a great athlete, no sports team would draft him because _____.
11. _____ because I watched a commercial.
12. The apartment complex was vacant because _____.
13. _____ so Hal bought a commercial building.
14. Shannon could not digest his food because _____.
15. _____ so we could not focus the microscope.
16. Because the Mint issued new state quarters, _____.

ACTIVITY 48 Test-Taking

Name: _____

Date: _____

Write the letter of the word that best matches the definition. Words can be used more than once.

a. coast	b. commercial	c. complex	d. debate	e. dice
f. digest	g. draft	h. exhaust	i. focus	j. issue

1. _____ a cold breeze felt inside a building
2. _____ a collection of previously published articles, essays, or reports
3. _____ a formal argument
4. _____ a matter of concern
5. _____ an area with many apartments or offices located together
6. _____ fumes from an engine
7. _____ game cubes
8. _____ moneymaking
9. _____ the area where land meets a large body of water
10. _____ the center or point of concentration
11. _____ to absorb or understand something
12. _____ to chop into small pieces
13. _____ to concentrate on something
14. _____ to glide down an incline without effort
15. _____ to produce something for distribution

ACTIVITY 49 Define Words That Are Easily Confused

Name:_____

Date:_____

Using the correct word can sometimes be tricky, especially when words look or sound almost alike. Match words with their definitions. Use a dictionary if you are unsure of the meaning of a word.

1. _____ advice
2. _____ advise
3. _____ ascent
4. _____ assent
5. _____ brake
6. _____ break
7. _____ choose
8. _____ chose
9. _____ device
10. _____ devise
11. _____ loose
12. _____ lose

a. selected
b. to think out, plan, or invent
c. not tight
d. to misplace something
e. shatter
f. information provided by someone
g. to rise
h. to agree
i. to select
j. to provide information, especially when making a decision
k. a device for stopping a vehicle
l. a machine or instrument

Select words from the list above.
13. Which word is the past tense of *choose*? _____
14. Which words are homophones? _____
15. Which words are verbs? _____

ACTIVITY 50 Use Words in Context

Name:_____

Date:_____

Circle the correct words to complete the sentences.

1. Be careful not to (brake / break) that expensive vase.
2. Before the hot air balloon began its (ascent / assent), passengers had to sign an (ascent / assent) form.
3. If you have any (loose / lose) items in your pockets, please put them in this bag so you do not (loose / lose) them while we are in the air.
4. Can you (device / devise) a way to keep us from drifting over the ocean?
5. Stop! Hit the (brake / break)!
6. The lawyer gave Milo good (advice / advise) about getting a patent for the (device / devise) he had invented.
7. Would you (advice / advise) us to select the pink or purple sofa?
8. Which would you (choose / chose)?
9. After much thought, we (choose / chose) the striped one.

ACTIVITY 51 Apply Vocabulary Words to Everyday Life

Name:_____

Date:_____

Answer the following questions on another sheet of paper.

1. Did you ever break anything valuable? What was it?
2. Would you like to try an ascent in a hot air balloon? Why or why not?
3. Did you ever lose anything important? What?
4. How do you apply the brakes on your bike?
5. If you could advise the president, what would you say?
6. If you could devise a plan for world peace, what would be the first step?
7. What color (other than white) would you choose to paint your room?
8. What is the best advice anyone ever gave you?
9. What new device would you like to invent? What would your new device do?
10. Which would you choose to see first at a zoo: the snakes or the birds?
11. What would you do if you found a large box of loose change in a park?
12. Would you give your assent for a trip to the moon? Why or why not?

ACTIVITY 52 Test-Taking

Name:_____

Date:_____

Circle "T" for true or "F" for false.

1. T   F   **Assent** means to agree.
2. T   F   To **loose** means to misplace something.
3. T   F   **Choose** means select.
4. T   F   You should apply the **brake** if you want to stop a car.
5. T   F   To **devise** means to think out, plan, or invent something.
6. T   F   You should tighten a screw that is **loose**.
7. T   F   To **advise** means to provide information for someone making a decision.
8. T   F   To **break** means to stop.
9. T   F   **Advice** is information provided by someone else.
10. T   F   **Ascent** means to agree.
11. T   F   A **devise** is a machine or instrument.
12. T   F   **Chose** means made a selection.

ACTIVITY 53 Review Words and Their Definitions

Name:_____

Date:_____

Match words with their definitions.

1. _____ acquire		a.	to do something you were told not to do; challenge; dare
2. _____ boulevard		b.	a place that sells cooked or prepared foods
3. _____ burrow		c.	to sit or stand with poor posture; slump
4. _____ campus		d.	the buildings and grounds of a school
5. _____ contradict		e.	the place to which a person or object is going
6. _____ defy		f.	a small alcove
7. _____ deli		g.	to get or obtain
8. _____ destination		h.	to go beyond the limits; take more than you should
9. _____ exceed		i.	a wide street with trees along the sides
10. _____ extinguish		j.	an underground home for an animal
11. _____ ignite		k.	to cause something to catch fire
12. _____ nook		l.	to put something off until later; delay
13. _____ oasis		m.	a place in the desert where there is water
14. _____ postpone		n.	to put out a fire
15. _____ slouch		o.	to say the opposite of what someone else says; oppose

ACTIVITY 54 Review Words and Their Definitions

Name:_____

Date:_____

Match words with their definitions.

1. _____ commercial		a.	very worried
2. _____ complex		b.	slowly decrease or run out
3. _____ debate		c.	the center or point of concentration
4. _____ draft		d.	moneymaking
5. _____ dwindle		e.	a cold breeze felt inside a building
6. _____ exhaust		f.	huge
7. _____ focus		g.	great; terrific
8. _____ frantic		h.	surprise, frighten, or alarm someone
9. _____ immense		i.	to misplace something
10. _____ issue		j.	unite, join, or bring together
11. _____ lose		k.	boring
12. _____ magnificent		l.	a matter of concern
13. _____ monotonous		m.	a formal argument
14. _____ startle		n.	fumes from an engine
15. _____ unify		o.	an area with many apartments or offices located together

27

ACTIVITY 55 Review Words and Their Definitions

Name:_____

Date:_____

Match words with their definitions.

1. _____ drawback
2. _____ gumshoe
3. _____ layaway
4. _____ petty
5. _____ ripcord
6. _____ showdown
7. _____ sideswipe
8. _____ significant
9. _____ spacious
10. _____ spendthrift
11. _____ subtle
12. _____ sufficient
13. _____ trendsetter
14. _____ turncoat
15. _____ versatile

a. able to do many things
b. enough; what is needed
c. a traitor
d. a slang term for a private detective
e. small; not important
f. one who spends money unwisely
g. to reserve an item by making a partial payment now
h. roomy; airy
i. important
j. a disagreement between two people or groups
k. problem; disadvantage
l. handle on a parachute that causes it to open
m. to strike along the side in passing
n. one who leads the way in fashion or another area
o. not obvious; slight

ACTIVITY 56 Review Words and Their Definitions

Name:_____

Date:_____

Match words with their definitions.

1. _____ advice
2. _____ advise
3. _____ ascent
4. _____ assent
5. _____ brake
6. _____ break
7. _____ choose
8. _____ chose
9. _____ device
10. _____ devise
11. _____ digest
12. _____ draft
13. _____ exhaust
14. _____ focus
15. _____ issue

a. selected
b. to think out, plan, or invent
c. to absorb or understand something
d. a machine or instrument
e. shatter
f. information provided by someone
g. to rise
h. to agree
i. a device for stopping a vehicle
j. to concentrate on something
k. to select
l. to provide information, especially when making a decision
m. to produce something for distribution
n. to select from a group for military service
o. to use up all of something

ACTIVITY 57 Define Nouns

Name:_____

Date:_____

Nouns name people, places, things, or ideas. All words on this list are nouns that name things.

Write nouns from the list to match the definitions. Use a dictionary if you are unsure of the meaning of a word.

accessories	barrier	brunch	capsule	infomercial
mural	parasites	pesticides	pulley	textiles

1. _____ a fence, wall, or other obstacle
2. _____ a painting of a scene on a wall
3. _____ a device consisting of a rope pulled over a wheel with a grooved rim to lift objects
4. _____ organisms that live off other beings
5. _____ a tablet or pill
6. _____ a long commercial in the format of a television program
7. _____ chemicals used to get rid of insects
8. _____ items made of cloth
9. _____ items worn with clothes, such as jewelry or a belt
10. _____ meal eaten late in the morning in place of breakfast and lunch

ACTIVITY 58 Use Personal Knowledge and Reference Sources

Name:_____

Date:_____

Write your answers to the questions below on another sheet of paper. Use a dictionary or other reference source if you need help.

1. Where is the Great Barrier Reef?
2. DDT is a pesticide. Why was DDT banned?
3. List ten items people might eat for brunch.
4. A capsule is a type of pill. What is another definition of *capsule*?
5. The small round circles on golf balls are called dimples. People have dimples too. Whom do you know who has dimples?
6. Why do you think companies make infomercials?
7. Fleas are parasites. Name two other types of parasites.
8. Name three appliances besides an oven and a dishwasher.
9. Name three types of accessories besides jewelry and belts.
10. Cotton and silk are two types of textiles. Name three others.
11. On your own paper, describe or draw a scene for a mural you would like to have on your bedroom wall.
12. On your own paper, explain in words or drawings how a pulley works.

29

ACTIVITY 59 Explore Vocabulary Words Name:_____

Date:_____

Use a dictionary if you need help with the answers
to the questions below.

1. Write the singular form of *accessories*. _____
2. What does *accessorize* mean? _____
3. What two words are shortened and combined to make the word *brunch*?
   _____ _____
4. What two words are shortened and combined to make the word *infomercial*?
   _____ _____
5. A capsule is a small container that encloses a dose of medicine. Of what material is the outer coating of a capsule made? _____
6. Why is it a good idea not to use pesticides around small children or pets?
   _____
7. Name one type of textile and how it's made. _____
   _____
8. Write three words that rhyme with *dimple*.
   _____ _____ _____
9. Which appliance in your home do you think is the most useful? _____
   Why? _____
10. How could fear of the dark be a mental barrier? _____
    _____

ACTIVITY 60 Test-Taking Name:_____

Date:_____

Write the letter of the best answer for each question.

1. _____ Which item is not an accessory?
   a. belt   b. tie   c. jewelry   d. shirt
2. _____ Which item is an appliance?
   a. hammer   b. pulley   c. refrigerator   d. telephone
3. _____ Which object is not a barrier?
   a. fence   b. a wall   c. mountain   d. pencil
4. _____ When do people eat brunch?
   a. late night b. early morning c. late morning   d. suppertime
5. _____ What is a dimple?
   a. a smile   b. a golf ball   c. a small depression   d. a hole in the ground
6. _____ Which two words were combined to make the word *infomercial*?
   a. information and commercial   b. inform and commerce
   c. advertisement and information   d. commercial and phone
7. _____ Which animal is a parasite?
   a. whale   b. bee   c. spider   d. flea
8. _____ Which task would you not use a pulley to complete?
   a. lift a heavy box   b. move a large stone
   c. push a wagon   d. pull up a fishing net
9. _____ Which item is not a textile?
   a. cotton   b. linen   c. wood   d. wool
10. _____ Which answer describes a mural?
    a. a wall   b. a large painted scene   c. a photograph   d. a small painting

30

ACTIVITY 61   Define Words With Suffixes   Name: _____

Date: _____

A **suffix** is added at the end of a word. It changes the meaning of the word. Sometimes the spelling of the root word changes also. When the suffix *-ment* is added to a verb, it changes the verb to a noun.

Answer the questions below. Use a dictionary if you are unsure of the meaning of a word.

1. To **require** means to need something. What does *requirement* mean?

    _____

2. To **achieve** means to reach a goal. What does *achievement* mean?

    _____

3. To **nourish** means to promote growth by feeding. What does *nourishment* mean?

    _____

4. To **harass** means to bother someone over and over. What does *harassment* mean?

    _____

5. To **enroll** means to sign up to join a class or school. What does *enrollment* mean?

    _____

6. To **command** means to order. What does *commandment* mean?

    _____

ACTIVITY 62   Use Words in Context   Name: _____

Date: _____

Write the singular or plural form of a word from the list to complete each sentence. Then write a brief answer to the question on another sheet of paper. Not all words will be used.

achieve	achievement	command	commandment	enroll	enrollment
harass	harassment	nourish	nourishment	require	requirement

1. What do you consider your best _____?

2. What are three things people need for _____?

3. What rule or _____ do you think is the most important for people to follow?

4. What goal would you like to _____ in the next 30 days?

5. What is the total _____ in your school?

6. What _____ from your parents do you think is the most reasonable?

7. What are three things everyone _____?

8. If you could _____ in any class, what kind would it be?

9. How do you react if someone _____ you?

10. What are the _____ for passing your next test?

ACTIVITY 63 Determine Fact or Opinion Name:_____

Date:_____

Circle "F" for fact or "O" for opinion.

1. F O All **commands** should be obeyed without question.
2. F O Everyone should be **required** to learn to play an instrument.
3. F O Everyone should **enroll** in a foreign language class.
4. F O Everyone should obey the Ten **Commandments**.
5. F O It is a **requirement** of most colleges that students first have a high school degree.
6. F O It should be against the law to **harass** someone.
7. F O One of Ben Franklin's **achievements** was the invention of bifocals.
8. F O I think people should feel proud when they **achieve** a goal.
9. F O People need food and liquid to **nourish** their bodies.
10. F O Plants need light, soil, and water for **nourishment**.
11. F O Some types of **harassment** are against the law.
12. F O The **enrollment** at Castle School declined last year.

ACTIVITY 64 Test-Taking Name:_____

Date:_____

Write the letter of the answer that best defines each word.

1. _____ enrollment
   a. a school   b. sign up
   c. number attending   d. students
2. _____ harass
   a. leave alone   b. to bother
   c. put a harness on   d. saddle a horse
3. _____ nourish
   a. eat   b. promote growth
   c. breakfast   d. food
4. _____ achievement
   a. a loss   b. a failure
   c. a command   d. a goal reached
5. _____ command
   a. to order   b. a law
   c. to ask   d. to know
6. _____ nourishment
   a. breakfast   b. requirement
   c. food needed to live d. meals
7. _____ achieve
   a. require   b. to reach a goal
   c. fail   d. encourage
8. _____ require
   a. to need   b. a request
   c. to desire   d. to wish
9. _____ commandment
   a. a request   b. an order
   c. to force   d. a list
10. _____ enroll
    a. begin   b. number
    c. student   d. sign up

ACTIVITY 65   Define Compound Words   Name:_____

Date:_____

A **compound word** combines two or more words to make a new word that expresses a single idea. Some compound words are hyphenated. Sometimes the meaning of the new word isn't clear, even though you know the meaning of both words used.

Draw a line to separate the compound words in the list into single words. Write words from the list to match their definitions. Use a dictionary if you are unsure of the meaning of a word.

forehand	freehand	high-handed	longhand	openhanded
shorthand	shorthanded	stouthearted	underhanded	

1. _____ bossy
2. _____ brave
3. _____ generous
4. _____ sneaky
5. _____ to draw or paint without a guide
6. _____ to write a letter, report, etc., with a pen or pencil
7. _____ understaffed; without enough help
8. _____ a system of writing quickly that uses symbols and shortened forms of words
9. _____ made or done with the hand moving palm forward

ACTIVITY 66   Form Additional Compound Words

Name:_____

Date:_____

Forehand, freehand, high-handed, longhand, openhanded, shorthand, shorthanded, and *underhanded* all contain the word *hand.*

Write ten or more compound words that also include the word *hand.* Use a dictionary or other source if you need ideas.

_____   _____   _____

_____   _____   _____

_____   _____   _____

_____   _____   _____

_____   _____   _____

On another sheet of paper, write definitions for ten of the words or use them in sentences to show you understand the meanings of the words.

ACTIVITY 67 Use Compound Words in Context

Name:_____

Date:_____

Write compound words from the list to complete the sentences.

forehand	freehand	high-handed	longhand	openhanded
shorthand	shorthanded	stouthearted	thumbtack	underhanded

1. Few people write letters in _____ anymore.
2. Some secretaries learn _____ so they can take notes quickly.
3. When Rachel acts so _____, she really upsets her friends.
4. Talking about someone behind her back is a very _____ thing to do.
5. Tobias is the most generous and _____ person I know.
6. Are you good at drawing _____?
7. The _____ knight set off on his quest for the missing princess.
8. Some of the police officers worked a double shift during the emergency because the department was _____.
9. Tina asked her tennis coach for help with her _____.
10. Please hand me a _____ so I can put this notice on the bulletin board.

ACTIVITY 68 Test-Taking

Name:_____

Date:_____

Circle "T" for true or "F" for false.

1. T F A person who is **stouthearted** needs to see a heart doctor soon.

2. T F A person who is **underhanded** is sneaky.

3. T F A **thumbtack** can be used for hanging heavy pictures on a wall.

4. T F Your **forehand** is the hand you use for writing.

5. T F **Shorthand** is a type of quick writing that uses symbols and abbreviations.

6. T F Someone who is **high-handed** is very bossy and acts like a snob.

7. T F To be **openhanded** means to drop things frequently.

8. T F To be **shorthanded** means one hand is shorter than the other.

9. T F To draw **freehand** means to follow a pattern.

10. T F When you write with a pen or pencil, you are writing

        in **longhand**.

ACTIVITY 69   Define Adjectives

Name:_____

Date:_____

Write the adjective from the list to match its definition. Use a dictionary if you are unsure of the meaning of a word.

capable	defiant	deliberate	hasty	hesitant
hostile	indifferent	jubilant	meek	unbearable

1. _____ able to do something; competent
2. _____ done in a hurried, careless way; rushed
3. _____ not caring; unconcerned; insensitive
4. _____ not obeying the rules; disobedient; rebellious
5. _____ shy or timid
6. _____ something that cannot be tolerated
7. _____ unfriendly or angry toward someone
8. _____ unsure about doing something; undecided
9. _____ very happy; feeling like celebrating; excited
10. _____ done on purpose, slowly, and carefully; planned

ACTIVITY 70   Write Antonyms and Synonyms for Adjectives

Name:_____

Date:_____

Write a synonym and an antonym for each word. Use a dictionary if you are unsure of the meaning of a word.

		Antonyms	**Synonyms**
1.	capable	_____	_____
2.	defiant	_____	_____
3.	hasty	_____	_____
4.	hesitant	_____	_____
5.	hostile	_____	_____

For each adjective, write two nouns the adjective could describe.

6.	capable	_____	_____
7.	defiant	_____	_____
8.	hasty	_____	_____
9.	hesitant	_____	_____
10.	hostile	_____	_____

ACTIVITY 71 Use Words in Context

Name:_____

Date:_____

Write a journal entry about something that happened in school.
Use at least five words from the list.

capable	defiant	deliberate	hasty	hesitant
hostile	indifferent	jubilant	meek	unbearable

_____

_____

_____

_____

_____

_____

_____

_____

ACTIVITY 72 Test-Taking

Name:_____

Date:_____

Write "A" if the words are antonyms. Write "S" if they are synonyms.

1. _____ acceptable and unbearable

2. _____ careful and deliberate

3. _____ competent and capable

4. _____ disobedient and defiant

5. _____ awful and unbearable

6. _____ hostile and meek

7. _____ uncaring and indifferent

8. _____ sad and jubilant

9. _____ timid and meek

10. _____ unfriendly and hostile

11. _____ careless and deliberate

12. _____ certain and hesitant

13. _____ concerned and indifferent

14. _____ friendly and hostile

15. _____ happy and jubilant

16. _____ hurried and hasty

17. _____ obedient and defiant

18. _____ slow and hasty

19. _____ unable and capable

20. _____ unsure and hesitant

ACTIVITY 73 Define Words With Multiple Meanings

Name:_____

Date:_____

The boldface words used below have several different meanings and can be used as more than one part of speech. They are used as nouns in the sentences. Write a short definition for each boldface word to match its use. Use a dictionary if you are unsure of the meaning of a word.

1. In most card games, the **ace** is the highest card. _____
2. The Gateway **Arch** in St. Louis is 630 feet high. _____
3. We bought an old Victrola at an **auction**. _____
4. Many fruit drinks are a **blend** of several different flavors. _____
5. The **boycott** against the bookstore lasted three months. _____
6. Maureen created beautiful designs on her **loom**. _____
7. One of the **perks** of working at the candy store is getting a discount.

_____

8. Pablo cooked pasta on the electric **range**. _____
9. Tex searched the **range** near the ranch for the missing cattle.

_____

10. Joanna planted hundreds of seeds, but so far, there is only one **sprout**.

_____

ACTIVITY 74 Define Words With Multiple Meanings

Name:_____

Date:_____

Write a definition for each word for the part of speech given.

1. ace (verb) _____
2. ace (adjective) _____
3. arch (verb) _____
4. arch (adjective) _____
5. auction (verb) _____
6. blend (verb) _____
7. boycott (verb) _____
8. loom (verb) _____
9. perk (verb) _____
10. range (verb) _____
11. sprout (verb) _____

ACTIVITY 75 Determine How Words Are Used

Name:_____

Date:_____

Review: Nouns are words that name people, places, things or ideas. **Verbs** are words that show action. **Adjectives** describe nouns.

Determine how the boldface word is used in each sentence. Write "N" if it is a noun, "V" if it is a verb, or "A" if it is used as an adjective.

1. _____ A pack of wolves may **range** over hundreds of square miles in the wilderness.
2. _____ Did you **ace** the test?
3. _____ Did you see the cat **arch** its back?
4. _____ Few people know how to weave cloth on a **loom**. It is almost a lost art.
5. _____ In 1962, the United States imposed a **boycott** on Cuban exports when Fidel Castro announced that Cuba had become a Communist state.
6. _____ The doctor told Paul his grandfather had a **terminal** illness.
7. _____ Joan bought a new **range** for her kitchen.
8. _____ Joel had a pair of **aces**.
9. _____ Seeds need water, soil, and light to **sprout**.
10. _____ Sherlock Holmes and Professor Moriarity were **arch** enemies.
11. _____ Some companies offer many benefits as **perks** for their employees.

ACTIVITY 76 Test-Taking

Name:_____

Date:_____

Determine how the boldface word is used in each sentence. Write "N" if it is a noun, "V" if it is a verb, or "A" if it is used as an adjective.

1. _____ The original words of *Home on the **Range*** were written by Dr. Brewster Higley in 1876.
2. _____ What will you get if you **blend** ice cream with strawberries?
3. _____ The seeds will **sprout** within two weeks.
4. _____ The threat of danger **loomed** over the hikers lost in the jungle.
5. _____ The train **terminal** was crowded last Saturday.
6. _____ We will **auction** off everything we don't need before we move to Florida.
7. _____ The Romans built many **arches**.
8. _____ Would you like to try a **blend** of peaches and cream?
9. _____ Would you **perk** some coffee for our guests?
10. _____ You can find many interesting items at an antique **auction**.
11. _____ The bus **boycott** in Montgomery, Alabama, began in 1955.
12. _____ Eddie Rickenbacker was the leading U.S. **ace** fighter pilot in World War I.

ACTIVITY 77   Define Words

Name: _____

Date: _____

Match words with their definitions. Use a dictionary if you are unsure of the meaning of a word.

1. _____ advantage
2. _____ appropriate
3. _____ competent
4. _____ conscious
5. _____ familiar
6. _____ formal
7. _____ legible
8. _____ practical
9. _____ tolerable
10. _____ satisfied

a. aware; deliberate; knowing
b. contented
c. writing that can be read
d. requiring fancy clothes and good manners
e. bearable; acceptable
f. correct or proper
g. sensible; handy; useful
h. well-known
i. benefit
j. capable; able

ACTIVITY 78   Add Prefixes/
Use Words in Context

Name: _____

Date: _____

When a **prefix** is added to the beginning of a word, the meaning of the word changes. Sometimes the spelling of the root word changes also. The prefixes *un-*, *dis-*, *in-*, *il-*, and *im-* change the meaning of a word to its opposite.

Add *un-*, *dis-*, *in-*, *il-*, or *im-* to each word. Write a short sentence on another sheet of paper for each new word that shows you understand the meaning of the word. Use a dictionary if you are unsure of the meaning or spelling of a word.

1. advantage
2. appropriate
3. competent
4. conscious
5. familiar

6. formal
7. legible
8. practical
9. satisfied
10. tolerable

ACTIVITY 79 Use Words in Context

Name:_____

Write words from the list that best complete the sentences.   Date:_____

> advantage   appropriate   conscious   disadvantage   formal   illegible
> impractical   inappropriate   informal   intolerable   legible   practical
> tolerable   unfamiliar

1. Family dinners are usually very friendly and _____.
2. Behavior that is _____ at home may be _____ at
   a fancy, _____ dinner.
3. One _____ of getting up early is watching the sun rise.
4. On the first day, Josh felt lost and at a _____ in the
   _____ surroundings of his new school.
5. If your writing is _____, you will need to practice to
   make it more _____.
6. A _____ use for a brick is as a doorstop, but that would
   be an _____ use for a feather.
7. Pam made a deliberate, _____ decision to help change the
   _____ situation in her neighborhood.
8. Only a small amount of sunlight was _____ for Shauna because of her
   sensitive skin.

ACTIVITY 80 Test-Taking

Name:_____

Date:_____

Write the letter of the answer that best matches the definition.

1. _____ aware   a. tolerable   b. conscious   c. intolerable   d. unconscious
2. _____ acceptable   a. intolerable   b. tolerable   c. satisfied   d. dissatisfied
3. _____ benefit   a. competent   b. incompetent   c. disadvantage   d. advantage
4. _____ capable   a. competent   b. appropriate   c. inappropriate d. incompetent
5. _____ contented   a. tolerable   b. satisfied   c. dissatisfied   d. intolerable
6. _____ correct   a. appropriate   b. inappropriate c. reasonable   d. unreasonable
7. _____ unreasonable   a. illegible   b. practical   c. informal   d. impractical
8. _____ difficulty   a. formal   b. advantage   c. disadvantage   d. informal
9. _____ well-known   a. legible   b. illegible   c. familiar   d. unfamiliar
10. _____ unaware   a. skilled   b. unconscious   c. conscious   d. unskilled
11. _____ unbearable   a. intolerable   b. suitable   c. unsuitable   d. tolerable
12. _____ strange   a. formal   b. unfamiliar   c. familiar   d. informal

ACTIVITY 81 Review Words and Their Definitions

Name: _____

Date: _____

Match the review words with their definitions.

1. _____ advantage
2. _____ accessories
3. _____ appropriate
4. _____ conscious
5. _____ defiant
6. _____ deliberate
7. _____ familiar
8. _____ formal
9. _____ hasty
10. _____ hesitant
11. _____ hostile
12. _____ indifferent
13. _____ jubilant
14. _____ legible
15. _____ meek

a. unfriendly or angry toward someone
b. not obeying the rules; disobedient; rebellious
c. done on purpose, slowly, and carefully; intentional; planned
d. uncaring
e. done in a hurried, careless way; rushed
f. writing that can be read
g. requiring fancy clothes and good manners
h. benefit
i. unsure about doing something; undecided
j. items worn with clothes, such as jewelry or a belt
k. well-known
l. sensible; handy; useful
m. shy; timid
n. aware; deliberate; knowing
o. very happy; feeling like celebrating; excited

ACTIVITY 82 Review Words and Their Definitions

Name: _____

Date: _____

Match the review words to their definitions.

1. _____ achieve
2. _____ achievement
3. _____ barrier
4. _____ brunch
5. _____ capsule
6. _____ command
7. _____ commandment
8. _____ dimple
9. _____ enroll
10. _____ harass
11. _____ infomercial
12. _____ mural
13. _____ nourish
14. _____ nourishment
15. _____ parasites

a. to reach a goal
b. a small pit or hole
c. a success
d. a rule or law
e. to promote growth by feeding
f. a type of pill
g. to sign up to join a class or school
h. meal eaten late in the morning in place of breakfast and lunch
i. to order
j. a painting of a scene on a wall
k. a fence, wall, or other obstacle
l. to bother someone over and over
m. organisms that live off other beings
n. a long commercial in the format of a television program
o. food for growth

ACTIVITY 83 Review Words and Their Definitions

Name: _____

Date: _____

Match the review words to their definitions.

1. _____ ace (adjective)
2. _____ ace (noun)
3. _____ appliances
4. _____ auction
5. _____ blend

6. _____ boycott
7. _____ forehand
8. _____ freehand
9. _____ high-handed
10. _____ longhand
11. _____ loom
12. _____ openhanded
13. _____ perk
14. _____ range
15. _____ tolerable

a. a bonus
b. bossy
c. done with the hand moving palm forward
d. to sell to the highest bidder
e. machines that do a special job to make life easier, such as a refrigerator or stove
f. a wide-open area
g. a refusal to deal with
h. usually the highest playing card in a deck
i. generous
j. bearable
k. to draw or paint without a guide
l. to combine several ingredients
m. to write a letter, report, etc., with a pen or pencil
n. first-rate
o. to come into view; to seem large

ACTIVITY 84 Review Words and Their Definitions

Name: _____

Date: _____

Match the review words to their definitions.

1. _____ ace
2. _____ arch (adjective)
3. _____ arch (noun)
4. _____ auction
5. _____ blend
6. _____ boycott
7. _____ loom
8. _____ perk (up)
9. _____ range (noun)
10. _____ range (verb)
11. _____ requirement
12. _____ shorthanded
13. _____ stouthearted
14. _____ terminal
15. _____ unbearable

a. an oven
b. a curved structure
c. to get more lively; wake up
d. a device for weaving cloth
e. a need
f. understaffed; without enough help
g. to wander freely; to roam
h. to get a high score
i. to refuse to buy from a place or use its services
j. a combination of two or more ingredients
k. final
l. a sale where people bid on items
m. brave
n. to bend backwards
o. something that cannot be tolerated

ACTIVITY 85 Define Nouns

Name:_____

Date:_____

Write the noun from the list to match its definition. Use a dictionary if you are unsure of the meaning of a word.

| buffet | dispenser | employer | fugitive | hermit | mansion |
| portrait | salon | siblings | spectator | suburb | vendor |

1. _____ a device that allows the contents to be removed and used in predetermined amounts
2. _____ a lifelike picture drawn or painted of a person
3. _____ a person or business that pays people to work; boss; supervisor
4. _____ a person who lives alone and doesn't like to be around people
5. _____ a place where people have their hair and nails done
6. _____ a seller; merchant
7. _____ an area where people live that is near or part of a larger city
8. _____ a very large, nice house; palace
9. _____ brothers and sisters
10. _____ meal where the food is set out and people help themselves
11. _____ one who flees from the law or other authority
12. _____ one who watches; a viewer

ACTIVITY 86 Classify Nouns

Name:_____

Date:_____

Nouns are words that name people, places, things, or ideas.

Write words from the list that fit into each group. Add other nouns of your own for each group.

	People	**Places**	**Things**
1. buffet	_____	_____	_____
2. dispenser	_____	_____	_____
3. employer	_____	_____	_____
4. fugitive	_____	_____	_____
5. hermit	_____	_____	_____
6. mansion	_____	_____	_____
7. portrait	_____	_____	_____
8. salon	_____	_____	_____
9. siblings	_____	_____	_____
10. spectator	_____	_____	_____
11. suburb	_____	_____	_____
12. vendor	_____	_____	_____

ACTIVITY 87 Use Nouns in Context/ Write Headlines

Name: _____

Date: _____

Use the singular or plural of each word to write an imaginary headline for a news story. Headlines should be six words or less. Use another sheet of paper if you need more room.

1. buffet _____

2. dispenser _____

3. employer _____

4. fugitive _____

5. hermit _____

6. mansion _____

7. portrait _____

8. salon _____

9. siblings _____

10. spectator _____

11. suburb _____

12. vendor _____

ACTIVITY 88 Test-Taking

Name: _____

Date: _____

Write the letter of the answer that best matches the definition.

1. _____ a device that allows something to be removed and used in predetermined amounts
   a. dispenser   b. vendor   c. dishwasher   d. refrigerator

2. _____ a lifelike picture drawn or painted of a person
   a. sketch   b. landscape   c. photograph   d. portrait

3. _____ a person or business that pays people to work
   a. employer   b. workers   c. employee   d. to hire

4. _____ a person who lives alone and doesn't like to be around people
   a. friend   b. hermit   c. sociable person   d. community

5. _____ a place where people have their hair, fingernails, and toenails done
   a. buffet   b. to cut hair   c. salon   d. hermitage

6. _____ a seller; merchant
   a. store   b. vendor   c. buyer   d. customer

7. _____ a smaller area where people live that is near or part of a much larger city
   a. suburb   b. metropolis   c. village   d. rural area

8. _____ a very large, nice house
   a. apartment   b. shanty   c. mansion   d. museum

ACTIVITY 89   Define Verbs

Name: _____

Date: _____

Write verbs from the list to match their definitions. Use a dictionary if you are unsure of the meaning of a word.

cater	condense	convey	dilate	emphasize	fidget
hover	impound	meander	meddle	shuffle	simmer

1. _____ to be restless; to squirm
2. _____ to express or relay a message
3. _____ to float in the air; to stay close
4. _____ to heat to a boil, then boil gently
5. _____ to make something smaller or shorter; to reduce
6. _____ to become wide
7. _____ to provide food and other items for someone's party
8. _____ to stress; to call attention to something
9. _____ to take something and keep it in legal custody
10. _____ to walk without lifting one's feet
11. _____ to wander in a meaningless direction
12. _____ to interfere with someone's business without permission

ACTIVITY 90   Use Verbs in Context

Name: _____

Date: _____

Write verbs from the list to complete the sentences.

convey	dilate	emphasize	fidget	hover
impound	meander	meddle	shuffle	simmer

1. When you see Greg, please _____ my congratulations on his graduation.
2. Brittany tried to _____ her point by using statistics in her presentation.
3. It's difficult not to _____ during a long plane ride.
4. Many small streams _____ across Minnesota.
5. Mia wanted the spaghetti sauce to _____ for several hours before dinner.
6. People who _____ are usually not appreciated.
7. Some people _____ their feet when they walk.
8. The police decided to _____ the car as evidence.
9. We watched the helicopter _____ over the ocean as they searched for sharks.
10. When there is little light, a cat's eyes _____ so it can see better.

ACTIVITY 91 Use the Past Tense of Verbs in Context

Name: _____

Date: _____

Past tense means something happened before now. For most verbs, add -ed to form the past tense. When verbs end in e, drop the e and add -ed. If a verb ends in a consonant and y, change the y to i and add -ed. (Do not change the y to i if a vowel comes before the y.)

Write a sentence using the past tense of each verb on another sheet of paper. Use a dictionary if you are unsure of a word.

1. cater
2. condense
3. convey
4. dilate
5. emphasize
6. fidget

7. hover
8. impound
9. meander
10. meddle
11. shuffle
12. simmer

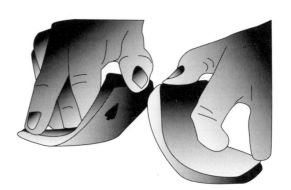

ACTIVITY 92 Test-Taking

Name: _____

Date: _____

Write "S" if the words are synonyms or "A" if they are antonyms.

1. _____ boil and simmer
2. _____ express and convey
3. _____ enlarge and dilate
4. _____ ignore and meddle
5. _____ reduce and condense
6. _____ remove and cater
7. _____ interfere and meddle
8. _____ reduce and dilate
9. _____ squirm and fidget
10. _____ stress and emphasize
11. _____ wander and meander

12. _____ enlarge and condense
13. _____ cool and simmer
14. _____ float and hover
15. _____ provide and cater
16. _____ release and impound
17. _____ seize and impound
18. _____ run and shuffle
19. _____ sit quietly and fidget
20. _____ stay still and meander
21. _____ take and convey
22. _____ zoom around and hover

ACTIVITY 93   Define Verbs

Name: _____

Date: _____

Write the word from the list to match its definition. Use a dictionary if you are unsure of the meaning of a word.

advance	amaze	confine	detach	encourage
enforce	enlarge	entertain	equip	retire

1. _____ to amuse or keep busy
2. _____ to astonish; surprise
3. _____ to give confidence; support
4. _____ to impose or require someone to obey
5. _____ to make something larger
6. _____ to move forward; to get a promotion
7. _____ to provide something needed
8. _____ to restrict or shut in
9. _____ to stop working at a paying job on purpose
10. _____ to take one part of a thing from another

OBSERVE
SCHOOL ZONE
20 mph

ACTIVITY 94   Add Suffixes to Change
Verbs to Nouns

Name: _____

Date: _____

When a suffix is added to the end of a word, it changes the meaning of the word. Sometimes the spelling of the root word also changes. The suffix *-ment* changes verbs to nouns.

Add the suffix *-ment* to each verb and write the noun. Write a brief definition for each noun. Use a dictionary if you are unsure of the meaning of a word.

Verb	Noun	Definition
1. advance	_____	_____
2. amaze	_____	_____
3. confine	_____	_____
4. detach	_____	_____
5. encourage	_____	_____
6. enforce	_____	_____
7. enlarge	_____	_____
8. entertain	_____	_____
9. equip	_____	_____
10. retire	_____	_____

47

ACTIVITY 95 Use Words in Context

Name: _____

Date: _____

Write words from the list to complete the sentences.

advance	advancement	amaze	amazement	enlarge	enlargement
entertain	entertainment	equip	equipment	retire	retirement

1. You can use a magnifying glass to _____ printing if it is too small to read.
2. What type of _____ do you enjoy most?
3. When Tim signed up for football, he needed all new _____.
4. We decided to _____ Jane's bike with training wheels until she learned to ride.
5. The game card said to _____ three spaces and lose a turn.
6. Although he had not studied, much to his _____, John got a 98% on the test.
7. The clown's favorite pastime was to _____ children at parties.
8. Sophie had an _____ made of her favorite photo.
9. My grandfather has spent his _____ fishing on the river.
10. Phil feels he has few chances for _____ in his current job.
11. Many people enjoy their hobbies more when they _____.
12. Look at this! It will truly _____ you.

ACTIVITY 96 Test-Taking

Name: _____

Date: _____

Write "S" if the words are synonyms or "A" if they are antonyms.

1. _____ working and retirement
2. _____ shock and amazement
3. _____ retire and withdraw
4. _____ reduction and enlargement
5. _____ equip and provide
6. _____ enlarge and decrease
7. _____ encourage and support
8. _____ detach and separate
9. _____ boredom and entertainment
10. _____ supplies and equipment
11. _____ retreat and advance
12. _____ release and confine

13. _____ freedom and confinement
14. _____ entertain and amuse
15. _____ enforce and impose
16. _____ detachment and attachment
17. _____ criticism and encouragement
18. _____ amaze and astonish

ACTIVITY 97 **Define Compound Words** Name:_____

Date:_____

A **compound word** combines two or more words to make a new word that expresses a single idea. Sometimes the meaning of the new word isn't clear, even though you know the meaning of both words used.

Write the compound word from the list to match its definition.

| barnstorm | downtrodden | dragnet | foresight | fortnight |
| freelance | gatecrasher | lukewarm | standoff | undermine |

1. a person who does jobs on a temporary "work for hire" basis _____
2. a systematic approach by police for catching suspects _____
3. a tie or draw, as in a contest; a contest that no one wins _____
4. an uninvited guest at a party _____
5. oppressed _____
6. not very warm; not very friendly _____
7. to look to the future by making plans in advance _____
8. to travel around the countryside making political speeches or presenting theatrical performances _____
9. to weaken by wearing away at a base or foundation _____
10. two weeks _____

ACTIVITY 98 **Critical Thinking** Name:_____

Date:_____

1. *Dragnet* was a popular, long-running radio (1949–1957) and television (1951–1959 and 1967–1970) police procedural show about the cases of a dedicated Los Angeles, California, police detective and his partners. Why was *Dragnet* a good name for a police show?

_____

2. Explain what you think this phrase means: "Hindsight is always better than foresight."

_____

3. In medieval times, soldiers or knights who were not bound to any lord or king were free to hire themselves out with their swords and lances as paid fighters. They became known as free lances. What is a lance? _____

4. List two advantages and two disadvantages of working as a freelancer (writer, computer programmer, graphic artist, consultant, etc.). _____

_____

5. What does the word *lop* mean?_____

6. Why do you think *lop* and *sided* were combined in *lopsided* to mean something that is shorter on one side than the other? _____

ACTIVITY 99 Use Compound Words in Context

Name: _____

Date: _____

Write a news article about a party. Use at least six words from this list in the article.

barnstorm	downtrodden	dragnet	foresight	fortnight	freelance
gatecrasher	hindsight	lopsided	lukewarm	standoff	undermine

Remember to answer the questions who, what, when, where, why, and how in your article.

_____

_____

_____

_____

_____

_____

_____

_____

ACTIVITY 100 Test-Taking

Name: _____

Date: _____

Write the letter of the word that would best replace the *** in each sentence.

1. _____ Our vacation lasted for a ***.
   a. barnstorm   b. foresight   c. hindsight   d. fortnight
2. _____ The police began a *** operation to catch the vandals.
   a. foresight   b. dragnet   c. hindsight   d. freelance
3. _____ If you would have had more ***, you would have realized what would happen.
   a. dragnet   b. freelance   c. foresight   d. hindsight
4. _____ Percy hoped there would be no *** at his exclusive party.
   a. gatecrashers   b. guests   c. visitors   d. fun
5. _____ When the child cut her own hair, it was very ***.
   a. lopsided   b. downtrodden   c. great   d. barnstorm
6. _____ The author of this book is a *** writer.
   a. lopsided   b. dragnet   c. barnstorm   d. freelance
7. _____ The tyrant kept the population *** and poor.
   a. happy   b. calm   c. downtrodden   d. lopsided
8. _____ You set a bad example for younger children when you *** the authority of officials.
   a. foresight   b. undermine   c. hindsight   d. gatecrasher
9. _____ With ***, it's easy to see what you could have done differently.
   a. foresight   b. hindsight   c. lukewarm   d. lopsided

ACTIVITY 101 Define Homophones

Name: _____

Date: _____

Homophones are words that sound the same, but have different meanings and spellings.

Write homophones to match the definitions. Some of these words may have more meanings than the one given below. Use a dictionary if you are unsure of the meaning of a word.

board	bored	peak	pique	principal	principle
reigns	reins	stationary	stationery	straight	strait

1. _____ when someone rules
2. _____ a piece of flat wood
3. _____ not crooked
4. _____ a law, belief, or rule
5. _____ highest point
6. _____ not interested
7. _____ to arouse anger or interest
8. _____ a leader or chief
9. _____ fancy paper for writing letters
10. _____ leather straps for guiding an animal
11. _____ a narrow space or passage
12. _____ not moving

ACTIVITY 102 Use Homophones in Context

Name: _____

Date: _____

Circle the correct homophones.

1. Arthur told me not to (peak / peek / pique) as we drove to the (peak / peek / pique) of the high hill.

2. His words (peaked / peeked / piqued) my interest, but I didn't (peek / peak / pique).

3. Shelly was a woman of strong (principles / principals).

4. The high school (principles / principals) all belonged to the city (Board / Bored) of Education.

5. My grandfather advised me to spend the interest if I needed money, but not to touch the (principle / principal).

6. Marco gets (board / bored) when he rides a (stationary / stationery) bike.

7. I bought lavender-scented (stationary / stationery) for my grandmother.

8. The king (reigns / reins), but the queen holds the (reigns / reins) of power.

9. If you travel (straight / strait) east, you will reach the (Straight / Strait) of Dover.

ACTIVITY 103 Write Rhymes

Name: _____

Date: _____

When writing rhymes for words with one syllable, you can also use words of two or more syllables. *Example:* Straight rhymes with debate, hesitate, and delegate.

When writing rhymes for words with two or more syllables, consider the whole word or only the last syllables of the word.
    Examples: Huckleberry, very, and Mary rhyme with stationary.

On another sheet of paper, list as many rhymes as you can for each set of words. Then write a sentence for each word using as many rhymes as you can.
    Example: Mary told Harry she bought Larry some very nice stationery.

board – bored

peak – pique

reigns – reins

stationary – stationery

straight – strait

ACTIVITY 104 Test-Taking

Name: _____

Date: _____

Write the letter of the answer that best matches the definition.

1. _____ a leader or chief   a. principal   b. principle
2. _____ not interested   a. board   b. bored
3. _____ not crooked   a. straight   b. strait
4. _____ most important   a. principal   b. principle
5. _____ flat piece of wood   a. board   b. bored
6. _____ an organized body of administrators   a. board   b. bored
7. _____ fancy paper for writing letters   a. stationary   b. stationery
8. _____ when someone rules   a. rains   b. reins   c. reigns
9. _____ arouse anger or interest   a. peak   b. peek   c. pique
10. _____ leather straps for guiding a. rains   b. reins   c. reigns
11. _____ highest point   a. peak   b. peek   c. pique
12. _____ a sum of money that earns interest   a. principal   b. principle
13. _____ a narrow waterway between landmasses   a. straight   b. strait
14. _____ a flat surface on which a game is played a. board   b. bored
15. _____ a truth, law, or moral outlook that   a. principal   b. principle
         governs behavior

52

ACTIVITY 105   Define Verbs

Name:_____

Date:_____

Match the verbs with their definitions. Use a dictionary if you are unsure of the meaning of a word.

1. _____ accumulate
2. _____ cancel
3. _____ comprehend
4. _____ duplicate
5. _____ extend
6. _____ occupy
7. _____ oppose
8. _____ supervise

a. to make an exact copy
b. to watch over someone
c. to call off; to stop
d. to make something larger or longer
e. to pile up or gather together
f. to understand something; to grasp
g. to live in a place; to take up space
h. to be against someone or something

ACTIVITY 106   Determine Root Words/ Define Words With Suffixes

Name:_____

Date:_____

Adding a **suffix** to the end of a word changes the meaning of the word. Sometimes the spelling of the root word also changes. Adding *-sion*, *-ation*, or *-tion* to a verb changes the word to a noun.

Write the verb that is the root word for each noun. Write a definition for each noun. Use a dictionary if you are unsure of the meaning of a word.

Verb Root Word	Noun	Definition of Noun
1. _____	accumulation	_____
2. _____	cancellation	_____
3. _____	comprehension	_____
4. _____	duplication	_____
5. _____	extension	_____
6. _____	occupation	_____
7. _____	opposition	_____
8. _____	supervision	_____

On another sheet of paper, write sentences using three or more of the nouns from the above list.

ACTIVITY 107 Apply Vocabulary Words to Personal Life

Name: _____

Date: _____

Write your answers to the following questions on another sheet of paper.

1. What types of things do you like to accumulate?

2. Is it possible to have too many accumulations? Explain your answer.

3. How do you feel when someone cancels plans you have made?

4. How do you feel when there is a school cancellation?

5. What occupation interests you?

6. What type of place would you like to occupy ten years from now?

7. Name one rule that you oppose.

8. On what do you base your opposition?

cancel

cancellation

oppose

opposition

ACTIVITY 108 Test-Taking

Name: _____

Date: _____

Write the letter of the answer that best defines each word.

1. _____ accumulate
2. _____ accumulation
3. _____ cancel
4. _____ cancellation
5. _____ comprehend
6. _____ comprehension
7. _____ duplicate
8. _____ duplication
9. _____ extend
10. _____ extension
11. _____ occupy
12. _____ occupation
13. _____ oppose
14. _____ opposition
15. _____ supervise
16. _____ supervision

a. to make something larger or longer
b. to gather
c. something that has been called off
d. those who are against you
e. direction; guidance
f. to make an exact copy
g. to live in a place
h. to call off; to stop
i. a job
j. to watch over
k. the process of copying something
l. to understand
m. understanding
n. to go against
o. an addition
p. a collection

54

ACTIVITY 109 Review Words and Their Definitions

Name:_____

Date:_____

Match the review words to their definitions.

1. _____ cater
2. _____ condense
3. _____ convey
4. _____ dispenser
5. _____ emphasize
6. _____ employer
7. _____ fidget
8. _____ hermit
9. _____ impound
10. _____ mansion
11. _____ salon
12. _____ siblings
13. _____ simmer
14. _____ suburb
15. _____ vendor

a. to take something and keep it in legal custody
b. a person who lives alone and doesn't like to be around people
c. to make something smaller or shorter; to reduce
d. a place where people have their hair, fingernails, and toenails done
e. a person or business that pays people to work; boss; supervisor
f. an area where people live that is near to or part of a larger city
g. to express or relay a message
h. to provide food and other items for someone's party
i. brothers and sisters
j. to stress; to call attention to something
k. to heat to a boil, then boil gently
l. a very large, nice house; palace
m. to be restless; to squirm
n. a seller; merchant
o. a device that allows the contents to be removed and used in predetermined amounts

ACTIVITY 110 Review Words and Their Definitions

Name:_____

Date:_____

Match the review words to their definitions.

1. _____ advance
2. _____ buffet
3. _____ confine
4. _____ detach
5. _____ dilate
6. _____ dragnet
7. _____ encourage
8. _____ entertain
9. _____ equip
10. _____ freelance
11. _____ meander
12. _____ meddle
13. _____ retire
14. _____ shuffle
15. _____ spectator

a. meal where the food is set out and people help themselves
b. to move forward; to get a promotion
c. to interfere with someone's business without permission; snoop
d. one who watches; a viewer
e. to walk without lifting one's feet
f. to give confidence; support
g. to take one part of a thing from another
h. to wander in a meaningless direction
i. to amuse or keep busy
j. to restrict or shut in
k. a systematic approach by police for catching suspects
l. to open wide; enlarge; expand
m. to provide something needed
n. a person who sells services to others on a "work for hire" basis
o. to stop working at a paying job on purpose

55

ACTIVITY 111 Review Words and Their Definitions

Name:_____

Date:_____

Match the review words to their definitions.

1. _____ board
2. _____ bored
3. _____ duplication
4. _____ occupation
5. _____ opposition
6. _____ peak
7. _____ pique
8. _____ principal
9. _____ principle
10. _____ reigns
11. _____ reins
12. _____ stationary
13. _____ stationery
14. _____ straight
15. _____ strait

a. those who are against you
b. fancy paper for writing letters
c. a channel; a narrow waterway between landmasses
d. a truth, law, or moral outlook that governs behavior
e. leather straps for guiding an animal
f. most important
g. to arouse anger or interest
h. not crooked
i. when someone rules
j. not interested
k. flat piece of wood
l. highest point
m. still; motionless
n. a job
o. the process of making a copy of something

ACTIVITY 112 Review Words and Their Definitions

Name:_____

Date:_____

Match the review words to their definitions.

1. _____ accumulate
2. _____ board
3. _____ cancellation
4. _____ comprehend
5. _____ downtrodden
6. _____ extend
7. _____ extension
8. _____ foresight
9. _____ gatecrasher
10. _____ hindsight
11. _____ lopsided
12. _____ lukewarm
13. _____ occupy
14. _____ supervise
15. _____ undermine

a. to make something larger or longer
b. to look to the future by making plans in advance
c. to weaken by wearing away at a base or foundation
d. to live in a place
e. to understand
f. oppressed
g. uneven; not balanced
h. an addition
i. to gather
j. something that has been called off
k. a flat surface on which a game is played
l. an uninvited guest at a party
m. understanding the nature of an event after it has happened
n. to watch over
o. not very warm; not very friendly

ACTIVITY 113 Define Verbs

Name: _____

Date: _____

Match the verbs with their definitions. Use a dictionary if you are unsure of the meaning of a word.

1. _____ admire
2. _____ determine
3. _____ evaluate
4. _____ exaggerate
5. _____ hesitate
6. _____ negotiate
7. _____ prohibit
8. _____ provoke
9. _____ reserve
10. _____ substitute

a. to describe something as better or worse than it really is
b. to set something aside
c. to decide; to conclude
d. to talk things over to try to reach an agreement; bargain
e. to take the place of
f. to forbid something
g. to appraise; to determine worth
h. to think highly of
i. to be uncertain; to pause
j. to irritate or anger someone; annoy

ACTIVITY 114 Add Suffixes/Define Words With Suffixes

Name: _____

Date: _____

Adding a suffix to the end of a word changes the meaning of the word. Sometimes the spelling of the root word also changes. Adding *-sion*, *-ation*, or *-tion* to a verb changes the word to a noun.

Add *-sion*, *-ation*, or *-tion* to each verb to make a noun. Write a brief definition for each noun. Use a dictionary if you need help with the definitions or spelling.

Verb Root Word	Noun	Definition of Noun
1. admire	_____	_____
2. determine	_____	_____
3. evaluate	_____	_____
4. exaggerate	_____	_____
5. hesitate	_____	_____
6. negotiate	_____	_____
7. prohibit	_____	_____
8. provoke	_____	_____
9. reserve	_____	_____
10. substitute	_____	_____

ACTIVITY 115 Use Words in Context/ Write Hyperboles

Name: _____

Date: _____

A **hyperbole** is a statement of exaggeration. "I must have walked 1,000 miles today!" is a hyperbole.

Use eight or more words from the list to write sentences that are hyperboles.

admiration	determine	determination	evaluate	evaluation	exaggerate
exaggeration	hesitate	hesitation	negotiate	negotiations	reservations
prohibition	provoke	provocation	prohibit	substitute	substitution

_____

_____

_____

_____

_____

_____

_____

_____

ACTIVITY 116 Test-Taking

Name: _____

Date: _____

Circle "T" for true or "F" for false.

1. T   F   A **provocation** is something that makes someone happy.
2. T   F   A **substitution** is something set aside.
3. T   F   **Admiration** is a verb.
4. T   F   An **evaluation** is a way to determine the value of something.
5. T   F   An **exaggeration** is a stretch of the truth.
6. T   F   **Substitute** means to replace one thing with another.
7. T   F   **Determine** means to decide.
8. T   F   **Exaggerate** is a noun.
9. T   F   **Hesitation** is a noun.
10. T   F   **Negotiations** are a type of bargaining.
11. T   F   **Prohibit** means something is not allowed.
12. T   F   To **negotiate** means to travel by water.
13. T   F   **Prohibition** means to appraise or evaluate.
14. T   F   **Reservations** means doubts about something.
15. T   F   Someone with **determination** has a strong purpose in life.

ACTIVITY 117 Define Easily Confused Words

Name:_____

Date:_____

Proper use of some words can be confusing. By knowing their definitions, you will be able to use them correctly. Write words from the list to match their definitions. Use a dictionary if you are unsure of the meaning of a word.

accept	affect	aggravate	all together	effect	bought
brought	continual	continuous	altogether	except	irritate

1. _____ means to act upon or influence.
2. _____ means repeated often.
3. _____ means to cause impatience, to provoke, or annoy.
4. _____ means without a stop.
5. _____ means to make a condition worse.
6. _____ is an adverb that means entirely, completely, or in all.
7. _____ means to accomplish something or bring about a result.
8. _____ means to agree to something or to receive something.
9. _____ is a phrase meaning everyone or everything in one place.
10. _____ is the past tense of *bring*.
11. _____ is the past tense of *buy.*
12. _____ means to exclude or hold something apart.

ACTIVITY 118 Determine the Correct Word

Name:_____

Date:_____

Circle the correct words to complete the sentences.

1. The coaches sat (altogether / all together) on the bench.
2. When the team lost, the coach was (aggravated / irritated).
3. Everyone agreed to the plan (accept / except) Hermione.
4. I ate (altogether / all together) too many hot peppers last night.
5. Is there a relationship between cause and (affect / effect)?
6. Jillian (bought / brought) balloons to the party that she (bought / brought) at the mall.
7. Miguel (accepted / excepted) his son's apology.
8. Scratching (aggravated / irritated) her rash.
9. The (affect / effect) of the new medication was amazing.
10. The (continual / continuous) interruptions affected my concentration.
11. The storm (affected / effected) the computer Internet service.
12. The (continual / continuous) sound of the surf lulls me to sleep at night.

ACTIVITY 119   **Use Words in Context/**   Name: _____
Write Questions   Date: _____

Write a question sentence using each word. Use correct punctuation.

1. accept _____
2. affect _____
3. aggravate _____
4. all together _____
5. altogether _____
6. bought _____
7. brought _____
8. continual _____
9. continuous _____
10. effect _____
11. except _____
12. irritate
13. Circle the number of one question, and then write the answer.

_____

ACTIVITY 120   **Test-Taking**   Name: _____

Date: _____

Write the letter of the answer that best matches the definition.

1. _____ to provoke or annoy   a. accept   b. irritate   c. aggravate   d. affect
2. _____ entirely, completely   a. altogether   b. alltogether   c. all together   d. except
3. _____ purchased   a. buyed   b. bought   c. brought   d. boughten
4. _____ past tense of *bring*   a. brought   b. bringed   c. bought   d. brung
5. _____ to accomplish   a. effect   b. irritate   c. except   d. affect
6. _____ without a stop   a. except   b. continual   c. continuous   d. accept
7. _____ to influence   a. effect   b. irritate   c. affect   d. aggravate
8. _____ to exclude   a. effect   b. accept   c. affect   d. except
9. _____ to agree   a. affect   b. except   c. irritate   d. accept
10. _____ in one place   a. except   b. altogether   c. all together   d. alltogether
11. _____ repeated often   a. effect   b. continual   c. affect   d. continuous
12. _____ to make a   a. irritate   b. aggravate   c. effect   d. except
      condition worse

ACTIVITY 121 **Define Nouns**

Name: _____

Date: _____

Match the nouns with their definitions. Use a dictionary
if you are unsure of the meaning of a word.

1. _____ autobiography
2. _____ majority
3. _____ gratuity
4. _____ duration
5. _____ epidemic
6. _____ biography
7. _____ census
8. _____ limitation
9. _____ hazard
10. _____ minority

a. set period of time
b. set amount
c. official counting of the population of a certain area
d. nonfiction account of one's own life
e. nonfiction account about the life of another person
f. more than half
g. less than half
h. dangerous place, situation, or item
i. a tip; money given to a person who performs a service
j. a disease that affects many people

ACTIVITY 122 **Use Nouns in Context**

Name: _____

Date: _____

Use words from the list to complete the sentences. If the sentence asks a question, answer the
question. Use your own paper if you need more room.

| autobiography | biography | census | duration | epidemic |
| gratuity | hazard | limitation | majority | minority |

1. Do you think people should leave a _____ when they eat at a restaurant?
   _____ Why or why not? _____

2. Do you think there should be any _____ on the movies you watch?
   _____ Why or why not? _____

3. For the _____ of the flu _____, health
   officials asked everyone to avoid crowds.

4. Is there a traffic _____ on the street where you live? _____

5. People who enjoy opera make up the _____ of the population.

6. There are 100 senators. How many are needed for a _____ vote? _____

7. What is the population of your city, according to the latest _____?
   _____

8. What would the first sentence of your _____ be? Write it on the
   back of this paper.

9. Whose _____ would you most like to read? _____

61

ACTIVITY 123 Use Reference Sources

Name:_____

Date:_____

Write the root words and a short definition. Use a dictionary if you are unsure of the meaning of a word. Use your own paper if you need more room.

	Root Word	Definition of Root Word
1.	limitation _____	_____
2.	majority _____	_____
3.	minority _____	_____

Use a dictionary or any other reference source.

4. The word *autobiography* is made up of three parts. "Auto" means self. "Bio" means life. What does "graphy" mean? _____

5. What does *biohazard* mean?_____

6. How often is the official U.S. census taken?_____

7. How are the words *duration* and *endure* the same? How are they different?_____

8. How are the words *gratuity* and *gratuitous* the same? How are they different?_____

ACTIVITY 124 Test-Taking

Name:_____

Date:_____

Write the letter of the answer that best matches the definition.

1. _____ a disease that affects many people
   a. duration   b. epidemic   c. colds   d. hazard

2. _____ a tip
   a. waitress   b. waiter   c. gratuity   d. majority

3. _____ dangerous place, situation, or item
   a. cave   b. hazard   c. traffic   d. poison

4. _____ less than half
   a. some   b. majority   c. many   d. minority

5. _____ more than half
   a. majority   b. minority   c. many   d. some

6. _____ nonfiction account about the life of another person
   a. adventure   b. biography   c. autobiography   d. novel

7. _____ nonfiction account of one's own life
   a. autobiography   b. fiction   c. realistic   d. biography

8. _____ official counting of the population of a certain area
   a. city   b. number   c. census   d. population

ACTIVITY 125 Define Words With Prefixes and Suffixes

Name:＿＿＿＿＿＿＿＿＿＿＿＿＿＿＿

Date:＿＿＿＿＿＿＿＿＿＿＿＿＿＿＿

A **prefix** is added to the beginning of a word. A **suffix** is added to the end of a word. Adding prefixes or suffixes to a word changes the meaning of the word.

The root words and their definitions are typed in bold. Use a dictionary to write a definition for all the other words. Underline the prefixes and suffixes.

1. **alter – to change**

   alteration＿＿＿＿＿＿＿＿＿＿＿＿＿＿＿＿＿＿＿＿＿＿＿＿＿＿＿＿＿＿＿＿＿＿＿＿＿＿＿

   alternate＿＿＿＿＿＿＿＿＿＿＿＿＿＿＿＿＿＿＿＿＿＿＿＿＿＿＿＿＿＿＿＿＿＿＿＿＿＿＿

   alternately＿＿＿＿＿＿＿＿＿＿＿＿＿＿＿＿＿＿＿＿＿＿＿＿＿＿＿＿＿＿＿＿＿＿＿＿＿＿

   alternative＿＿＿＿＿＿＿＿＿＿＿＿＿＿＿＿＿＿＿＿＿＿＿＿＿＿＿＿＿＿＿＿＿＿＿＿＿＿

   unaltered＿＿＿＿＿＿＿＿＿＿＿＿＿＿＿＿＿＿＿＿＿＿＿＿＿＿＿＿＿＿＿＿＿＿＿＿＿＿

2. **consider – to think about; to ponder**

   considerable＿＿＿＿＿＿＿＿＿＿＿＿＿＿＿＿＿＿＿＿＿＿＿＿＿＿＿＿＿＿＿＿＿＿＿＿

   consideration＿＿＿＿＿＿＿＿＿＿＿＿＿＿＿＿＿＿＿＿＿＿＿＿＿＿＿＿＿＿＿＿＿＿＿

   inconsiderate＿＿＿＿＿＿＿＿＿＿＿＿＿＿＿＿＿＿＿＿＿＿＿＿＿＿＿＿＿＿＿＿＿＿＿

   reconsider＿＿＿＿＿＿＿＿＿＿＿＿＿＿＿＿＿＿＿＿＿＿＿＿＿＿＿＿＿＿＿＿＿＿＿＿＿

ACTIVITY 126 Use Words in Context

Name:＿＿＿＿＿＿＿＿＿＿＿＿＿＿＿

Date:＿＿＿＿＿＿＿＿＿＿＿＿＿＿＿

Write words from the list to complete the sentences.

alteration	alternate	alternative	considerable	consideration	cooperation
cooperative	detective	detector	inconsiderate	reconsider	undetectable

1. The ＿＿＿＿＿＿＿＿＿＿＿ spent a ＿＿＿＿＿＿＿＿＿＿＿ amount of time searching for the missing jewels.

2. If you do not have a smoke ＿＿＿＿＿＿＿＿＿＿＿ in your home, you should ＿＿＿＿＿＿＿＿＿＿＿ that decision.

3. It will take ＿＿＿＿＿＿＿＿＿＿＿ by scientists to find an ＿＿＿＿＿＿＿＿＿＿＿ source of fuel for the future.

4. Have you taken into ＿＿＿＿＿＿＿＿＿＿＿ all the ＿＿＿＿＿＿＿＿＿＿＿ options?

5. The ＿＿＿＿＿＿＿＿＿＿＿ to the bride's wedding gown was ＿＿＿＿＿＿＿＿＿＿＿ to the guests.

6. People who are ＿＿＿＿＿＿＿＿＿＿＿ of others are also usually not very ＿＿＿＿＿＿＿＿＿＿＿ either.

ACTIVITY 127 Apply Knowledge of Vocabulary Words to Everyday Life

Name: _____

Date: _____

Answer the following questions on another sheet of paper.

1. If you could make an alteration to the place where you live, what would you change?

2. What are two alternate options for something fun to do on a Saturday?

3. Who do you know that is most likely to seriously consider your opinion?

4. How do you react to people who are inconsiderate?

5. What do you spend considerable energy doing?

6. What do you take into consideration when deciding which book to read?

7. If you could alter one thing about yourself, what would it be?

8. Name a person who is very cooperative.

9. How do you react to uncooperative people?

10. Would you like to be a private detective? Why or why not?

11. How many smoke detectors do you have where you live?

ACTIVITY 128 Test-Taking

Name: _____

Date: _____

Write the letter of the answer that best matches the definition.

1. _____ a great amount
   a. alternative   b. consider
   c. considerable   d. consideration

2. _____ a joint effort
   a. consider   b. cooperate
   c. cooperation   d. cooperative

3. _____ on the other hand
   a. alter   b. alteration
   c. alternate   d. alternately

4. _____ selfish
   a. inconsiderate   b. reconsider
   c. considerable   d. consideration

5. _____ think again
   a. inconsiderate   b. reconsider
   c. considerable   d. consideration

6. _____ exchange
   a. alter   b. alteration
   c. alternate   d. alternately

7. _____ find
   a. detect   b. detection
   c. detective   d. detector

8. _____ to help
   a. uncooperative   b. cooperate
   c. cooperation   d. cooperative

ACTIVITY 129 Define Homophones

Name:_____

Date:_____

Homophones are words that sound the same but have different meanings and spellings. Write the homophones to match the definitions. Use a dictionary if you are unsure of the meaning of a word.

bouillon	bullion	canapé	canopy	complement	compliment
humerus	humorous	pedal	peddle	residence	residents

1. I am a covering that blocks the sun. What word am I?   _____
2. I am a clear liquid made from boiling meat. What word am I?   _____
3. I am a place where people live. What word am I?   _____
4. I am a snack served before a meal. What word am I?   _____
5. I am a verb that means *to sell*. What word am I?   _____
6. I am an expression of praise or congratulations. What word am I?   _____
7. I am another word for *funny*. What word am I?   _____
8. I am part of a bicycle. What word am I?   _____
9. I am people who live in a specific place. What word am I?   _____
10. I am the long bone in your arm. What word am I?   _____
11. I am very valuable because I am bars of gold. What word am I?   _____
12. I complete, make whole, or bring to perfection. What word am I?   _____

ACTIVITY 130 Use Homophones in Context

Name:_____

Date:_____

Circle the correct words to complete the sentences.

1. A large amount of the United States' gold reserves is stored in the vault of the Fort Knox (Bouillon / Bullion) Depository.
2. At one time, people bought pots, pans, needles, and other small items from traveling (pedalers / peddlers).
3. The (canapé / canopy) of the rain forest was filled with colorful birds and chattering monkeys.

4. Brad fell off his bike when a (pedal / peddle) broke and, sadly, he broke his (humerus / humorous) bone.
5. All the elderly (residence / residents) of the retirement (residence / residents) enjoyed the (canapés / canopies) we brought to the party.
6. They (complemented / complimented) us on the (bouillon / bullion) prepared by the cooking class.
7. They said the seasonings (complemented / complimented) the flavor.
8. No one thought Brittany's jokes were very (humerus / humorous).
9. Maria (pedaled / peddled) her bike to school every day.

ACTIVITY 131 Critical Thinking

Name: _____

Date: _____

Write short bits of dialogue between two people in which one person is thinking of one word and the other is thinking of the word that is its homophone. Use at least four pairs of homophones from the list.

Example: Gus: Let's have bouillon for lunch.
        Henry: No thanks. I can't chew gold bullion with my false teeth.

bouillon	bullion	canapé	canopy	complement	compliment
humerus	humorous	pedal	peddle	residence	residents

_____

_____

_____

_____

_____

_____

_____

ACTIVITY 132 Test-Taking

Name: _____

Date: _____

Write the letter of the answer that matches the definition.

1. _____ These are people: a. residence   b. residents
2. _____ This is edible: a. bouillon   b. bullion
3. _____ This is expensive: a. bouillon   b. bullion
4. _____ This is funny: a. humerus   b. humorous
5. _____ This is nice to hear: a. complement   b. compliment
6. _____ This is edible: a. canapé   b. canopy
7. _____ This is a place: a. residence   b. residents
8. _____ This is not edible: a. canapé   b. canopy
9. _____ This is on a bike: a. pedal   b. peddle
10. _____ This provides shade: a. canapé   b. canopy
11. _____ This means to sell: a. pedal   b. peddle
12 _____ This isn't funny; it's a bone: a. humerus   b. humorous
13. _____ This is one of two angles: a. complementary   b. complimentary

ACTIVITY 133 Define Compound Words

Name:_____

Date:_____

A **compound word** combines two or more words to make a new word that expresses a single idea. Draw a line to separate the compound words in the list into single words. Write words from the list to match their definitions. Use a dictionary if you are unsure of the meaning of a word.

carryover	earthwork	fanfare	flagstone	foreground	haywire
keepsake	light-headed	milestone	pussyfoot	safeguard	workhorse

1. _____ a flat slab of stone used for walkways
2. _____ a signpost marking distance; an important event in one's life
3. _____ a wall or barrier made of dirt
4. _____ dizzy; faint
5. _____ a flourish; showy display
6. _____ memento; a token whose main value is sentimental
7. _____ not working correctly; broken
8. _____ one who is a hard worker
9. _____ postponement until later
10. _____ the part of a picture that appears closest to the viewer
11. _____ to protect; a protection against danger
12. _____ to move cautiously; to avoid giving a definite answer

ACTIVITY 134 Use Compound Words in Context

Name:_____

Date:_____

Write the correct word from the list to fill in the blank.

carryover	earthworks	foreground	keepsake	light-headed
milestone	pussyfoot	safeguards	workhorse	

1. When Jessie was sick, she couldn't eat for several days and felt very _____.

2. Esau kept the shiny, smooth, black river rock as a _____ of the time he and his dad first went fishing.

3. The _____ of my favorite painting is solid red.

4. In some companies, if you don't use all of your vacation days, you can take them as a _____ for the next year.

5. Make up your mind, Terry. Don't _____ around all day.

6. People often called Stanley when they needed help because he is a real _____.

7. The birth of a child is a joyous _____ in most families.

8. The Civil War Club members built _____ before they reenacted a famous battle.

9. The machine was dangerous because it had no _____.

ACTIVITY 135　Use Words in Context/ Apply Personal Knowledge

Name:_____

Date:_____

Answer the following questions on another sheet of paper.

1. Whom do you know who could be considered a workhorse?

2. Why do you think soldiers build earthworks?

3. What musical instruments do you think are appropriate for a fanfare?

4. Describe a place where you have seen flagstones.

5. Describe a time when something went haywire and what you did about it.

6. List some items people might consider as keepsakes.

7. Have you ever known anyone to become light-headed? What caused it?

8. Describe the most important milestone in your life so far.

9. How do you feel about people who pussyfoot around and won't give you a definite answer or make a commitment?

10. Suggest a safeguard that would make your life safer.

ACTIVITY 136　Test-Taking

Name:_____

Date:_____

Write the letter of the definition that best matches the word.

1. _____ workhorse
2. _____ safeguard
3. _____ pussyfoot
4. _____ milestone
5. _____ light-headed
6. _____ keepsake
7. _____ haywire
8. _____ foreground
9. _____ flagstone
10. _____ fanfare
11. _____ earthwork
12. _____ carryover

a. a flat slab of stone used for walkways

b. a signpost marking distance; an important event in one's life

c. a wall or barrier made of dirt

d. dizzy; faint

e. a flourish; showy display

f. memento; a token whose main value is sentimental

g. not working correctly; broken

h. one who is a hard worker

i. postponement until later

j. the part of a picture that appears closest to the viewer

k. to protect; a protection against danger

l. to move stealthily or cautiously; to avoid giving a definite answer

ACTIVITY 137 Review Words and Their Definitions

Name: _____

Date: _____

Match the review words to their definitions.

1. _____ admire
2. _____ affect
3. _____ aggravate
4. _____ altogether
5. _____ continual
6. _____ continuous
7. _____ determine
8. _____ effect
9. _____ evaluate
10. _____ exaggerate
11. _____ hesitate
12. _____ prohibit
13. _____ provoke
14. _____ reserve
15. _____ substitute

a. repeated often
b. to irritate or anger someone; annoy
c. to forbid something
d. to decide; to conclude
e. to think highly of
f. to take the place of
g. to set something aside
h. entirely, completely, or in all
i. without a stop
j. to accomplish something or bring about a result
k. to act upon or influence
l. to describe something as better or worse than it is
m. to appraise; to determine worth
n. to make a condition worse
o. to be uncertain; to pause

Teacher's Evaluation

ACTIVITY 138 Review Words and Their Definitions

Name: _____

Date: _____

Match the review words to their definitions.

1. _____ accept
2. _____ alternately
3. _____ autobiography
4. _____ biography
5. _____ bought
6. _____ brought
7. _____ considerable
8. _____ cooperative
9. _____ duration
10. _____ epidemic
11. _____ except
12. _____ gratuity
13. _____ hazard
14. _____ limitation
15. _____ majority

a. to agree to something or to receive something
b. to exclude or hold something apart
c. the past tense of *buy*
d. the past tense of *bring*
e. set amount
f. a great amount
g. a joint effort
h. set period of time
i. more than half
j. on the other hand
k. a disease that affects many people
l. nonfiction account of one's own life
m. nonfiction account about the life of another person
n. dangerous place, situation, or item
o. a tip; money given to a person who performs a service

ACTIVITY 139 Review Words and Their Definitions

Name: _____

Date: _____

Match the review words to their definitions.

1. _____ alter
2. _____ alternate
3. _____ bouillon
4. _____ canapé
5. _____ canopy
6. _____ compliment
7. _____ cooperate
8. _____ detect
9. _____ humorous
10. _____ inconsiderate
11. _____ pedal
12. _____ peddle
13. _____ reconsider
14. _____ unaltered
15. _____ undetectable

a. to change back and forth between two or more things
b. unnoticeable
c. to sell
d. unchanged
e. to work together
f. a snack served before a meal
g. think again
h. selfish
i. a covering that blocks the sun
j. an expression of praise or congratulations
k. funny
l. the part of a bicycle a rider pushes to make it go
m. a clear liquid made from boiling meat
n. to make a change
o. to find

ACTIVITY 140 Review Words and Their Definitions

Name: _____

Date: _____

Match the review words to their definitions.

1. _____ bullion
2. _____ carryover
3. _____ complement
4. _____ consider
5. _____ considerable
6. _____ detective
7. _____ earthwork
8. _____ fanfare
9. _____ flagstone
10. _____ foreground
11. _____ haywire
12. _____ humerus
13. _____ keepsake
14. _____ light-headed
15. _____ milestone

a. something left over
b. a signpost marking distance; an important event in one's life
c. the long bone in your arm
d. flourish; a showy display
e. a flat slab of stone used for walkways
f. dizzy; faint
g. not working correctly; broken
h. the part of a picture that appears closest to the viewer
i. to complete, make up a whole, or bring something to perfection
j. a wall or barrier made of dirt
k. bars of gold
l. police officer; private investigator
m. to think about; to ponder
n. very much
o. memento; a token of which the main value is sentimental

ACTIVITY 141   Define Words With Prefixes and Suffixes

Name:_____

Date:_____

A **prefix** is added to the beginning of a word. A **suffix** is added to the end of a word. Adding a prefix and/or suffix to a word changes the meaning of the word. Sometimes the spelling of the root word also changes.

The root words and their definitions are typed in bold. Use a dictionary to write a definition for all the other words. Underline the prefixes and suffixes.

1. **direct – to lead**
    direction _____
    directive _____
    directly _____
    director _____
    directory _____
    misdirection _____

2. **invest – to put something (time, money, energy, etc.) into something in the hope that it will pay off later**
    investigate _____
    investigation _____
    investigator _____
    investor _____
    reinvest _____

ACTIVITY 142   Use Words in Context

Name:_____

Date:_____

Use words from the list to complete the sentences.

direct	directly	director	directory	investigate	investigation	investigator
investors	observant	observation	observatory	proposal	proposed	

1. "I will be with you _____," said the _____ of the astronomy _____ to the private _____ hired to find the missing stars.

2. "Geoffrey is very _____; he noticed that several stars listed in the _____ are missing," he explained.

3. "One of the _____ in this great institution _____ that we hire you to _____ the problem."

4. "We hope you will accept our _____ and begin the _____ at once."

5. "I can _____ you to the best _____ point so you can begin."

ACTIVITY 143 Differentiate Between Nouns and Verbs

Name:_____

Date:_____

Write "N" if the word is a noun or "V" if it is a verb.

1. _____ direct
2. _____ directive
3. _____ directory
4. _____ investigate
5. _____ investigator
6. _____ observance
7. _____ observatory
8. _____ observer
9. _____ propose
10. _____ reinvest

11. _____ direction
12. _____ director
13. _____ invest
14. _____ investigation
15. _____ investor
16. _____ observation
17. _____ observe
18. _____ proposal
19. _____ proposition

ACTIVITY 144 Test-Taking

Name:_____

Date:_____

Circle "T" for true or "F" for false.

1. T   F   A **directive** is an order or command.
2. T   F   A **directory** is a book of directions.
3. T   F   A **proposition** is a suggestion or plan.
4. T   F   An **investor** is one who wears vests.
5. T   F   **Direct** means to act in a play.
6. T   F   To **observe** means to watch or look at.
7. T   F   A **director** is one who leads.
8. T   F   An **observatory** is a place where people watch movies.
9. T   F   To **reinvest** means to wear a vest two days in a row.
10. T   F   **Directions** can mean points on a compass or instructions.
11. T   F   An **investigation** is a study of something.
12. T   F   **Misdirection** means to get lost.
13. T   F   **Observance** of a holiday means to celebrate it.
14. T   F   To be **observant** means to pay attention to details.
15. T   F   A **proposal** is a promise.
16. T   F   To **investigate** means to look into something.

ACTIVITY 145 Define Compound Words

Name:_____

Date:_____

Draw a line to separate the compound words in the list into single words. Write words from the list to match their definitions. Use a dictionary if you are unsure of the meaning of a word.

doughboy	flagship	highbrow	jitterbug	ladyfinger
oversight	sandhog	tableland	undercoat	undertow

1. _____ a flat, elevated area of land; a plateau or mesa
2. _____ a slang term for an American foot soldier in World War I
3. _____ a strenuous dance performed to quick-tempo swing or jazz music consisting of various two-step patterns with twirls and other acrobatic maneuvers
4. _____ a type of dessert; a small finger-shaped sponge cake
5. _____ failure to notice
6. _____ one who works inside a watertight structure while building underwater tunnels
7. _____ primer; sealing material applied to a surface before painting
8. _____ highly cultured or intellectual
9. _____ the seaward pull of receding waves after they break on shore
10. _____ a ship that carries the commander of a fleet and flies his flag

ACTIVITY 146 Explore Alternate Meanings/Apply Personal Experience

Name:_____

Date:_____

Use a reference source and personal experience to answer the questions.

1. On an animal, what is an undercoat? _____
2. Beside being a term for a soldier, what is another, completely different meaning of dough-boy? _____
3. What activities do you consider highbrow? _____
4. Why is it a good idea not to jaywalk? _____
   _____
5. Why do you think the words *table* and *land* were combined to describe a flat, elevated area of land? _____
6. What is dangerous about an undertow? _____
7. At one time, dance marathons where couples did the jitterbug and other types of dances were very popular. What was a dance marathon? _____
   _____

   Would you like to participate in a dance marathon? _____ Why or why not?
   _____

8. Would you like a job as a sandhog? _____ Why or why not? _____
   _____

ACTIVITY 147 Use Compound Words in Context/Write Headlines

Name:_____

Date:_____

Use the singular or plural of each word to write an imaginary headline for a news story. Headlines should be six words or less. Use another sheet of paper if you need more room.

1. doughboy _____
2. flagship _____
3. forewarn _____
4. highbrow _____
5. jaywalk _____
6. jitterbug _____
7. ladyfinger _____
8. oversight _____
9. sandhog _____
10. tableland _____
11. undercoat _____
12. undertow _____

ACTIVITY 148 Test-Taking

Name:_____

Date:_____

Circle "T" for true or "F" for false.

1. T F A **jitterbug** is a rare insect found only in tropical rain forests.
2. T F A **sandhog** works high in the air on a tall ladder or pole.
3. T F A **highbrow** is a person who plucks her eyebrows.
4. T F A **jitterbug** is a fast-paced dance.
5. T F A **ladyfinger** is a type of dessert.
6. T F A **sandhog** is a pig without a mud puddle.
7. T F A **doughboy** is a person learning to become a baker.
8. T F An **oversight** is a failure to notice something important.
9. T F An **undertow** is a large wave that surfers ride to shore.
10. T F **Doughboy** is a slang term for a person with lots of money.
11. T F **Forewarn** means to warn in advance.
12. T F **Oversight** means to peer over the top of bifocals.
13. T F **Tableland** is another word for a mesa or plateau.
14. T F A **flagship** carries the fleet commander's flag.
15. T F To **forewarn** means to give four warnings.
16. T F To **jaywalk** means to walk like a blue jay.
17. T F To **undercoat** means to paint the inside of a jacket.

ACTIVITY 149   Define Number Words

Name: _____

Date: _____

Use a dictionary or other reference source to answer the questions.

1. **Twins** are two children born to the same mother at the same time.
    What are **quadruplets**? _____

2. There are three musicians in a **trio**.
    How many are in a **quartet**? _____
    How many are in a **quintet**? _____

3. How many notes are in an **octave**? _____

4. How many legs does a **tripod** have? _____

5. How many events are in a **pentathlon**? _____

6. How many wheels does a **unicycle** have? _____

7. How many events are in a **decathlon**? _____

8. How many languages does a person speak if he is **bilingual**? _____

9. How many years are in a **decade**? _____

10. How many years are in a **century**? _____

11. How many years are in a **millennium**? _____

12. A **centennial** is an event that occurs once in 100 years.
    How often does a **bicentennial** occur? _____

13. How often does a **sesquicentennial** event occur? _____

ACTIVITY 150   Use Number Prefixes
to Make New Words

Name: _____

Date: _____

Parts of words that denote a number usually come from Latin or Greek words.

For each word part listed, write three or more words. Use a dictionary or other reference source if you need help.

1. *uni-* means 1 _____

2. *bi-* means 2 _____

3. *tri-* means 3 _____

4. *quad-* means 4 _____

5. *quin-* means 5 _____

6. *penta-* means 5 _____

7. *oct-* means 8 _____

8. *dec-* means 10 _____

9. *cent-* means 100 _____

10. *milli-* means 1,000 _____

ACTIVITY 151 **Use Words With Number Prefixes in Context**

Name:_____

Date:_____

Write three words that use "quad-" or "oct-" as part of the word. Write a sentence using each of the words.

1. _____
   _____

2. _____
   _____

3. _____
   _____

Write three words that use "tri-" or "penta-" as part of the word. Write a definition for each word.

4. _____
   _____

5. _____
   _____

6. _____
   _____

ACTIVITY 152 **Test-Taking**

Name:_____

Date:_____

Write the letter of the answer that is the best definition for each word.

1. _____ bicentennial   a. 200 musicians   b. 200 people
                         c. 200 years   d. 20 years

2. _____ bilingual   a. 2 wheels   b. 2 languages
                         c. twins   d. 2 weeks

3. _____ century   a. 10 years   b. 100 years
                         c. 100 days   d. 100 minutes

4. _____ decade   a. 10 events   b. 100 years
                         c. 10 years   d. 10 musicians

5. _____ decathlon   a. 10 years   b. 10 wheels
                         c. 10 of a kind   d. 10 events

6. _____ millennium   a. 100 years   b. 1,000 years
                         c. 10 years   d. 150 years

7. _____ octave   a. 8 notes   b. 80 notes
                         c. 8 musicians   d. 8 years

8. _____ pentathlon   a. 5 weeks   b. 5 events
                         c. 5 of a kind   d. 5 years

9. _____ quadruplets   a. 4 of the same   b. 4 musicians
                         c. 4 years   d. 40 years

10. _____ quintet   a. 5 wheels   b. pentagon
                         c. 5 musicians   d. 4 musicians

76

ACTIVITY 153 Identify Mythological/
Legendary Creatures

Name:_____

Date:_____

Match the names of these creatures from myths and legends with their definitions. Use a dictionary if you are unsure of the meaning of a word.

> basilisk   centaur   chimera   dryad   harpy   mermaid
> minotaur   naiad   phoenix   satyr   sphinx

1. _____ a bird that lived for 500 years, then burst into flames and was reborn from the ashes
2. _____ a creature with the head and upper body of a woman and the lower body of a lion
3. _____ a creature with the head and arms of a human and body of a horse
4. _____ a creature with the upper body of a man and lower body of a goat
5. _____ a creature with the head and upper body of a woman and wings and lower body of a vulture
6. _____ a creature with the upper part of a woman and lower part of a fish
7. _____ a fire-breathing creature that was part lion, goat, and serpent
8. _____ a reptilian creature that turned people to stone
9. _____ a tree nymph
10. _____ a water nymph
11. _____ a creature with the body of a man and the head of a bull

ACTIVITY 154 Explore Mythological
Words

Name:_____

Date:_____

Use any reference sources to find the answers to these questions.

1. Which major city in Arizona was named for a mythological creature? _____
2. On what island did the **minotaur** live? _____
3. What was unique about the place where the **minotaur** lived?_____
4. In mythology, who destroyed the minotaur? _____
5. The **sphinx** was a creature in both Egyptian and Greek mythology. Where is the famous monument known as the Great Sphinx located? _____
6. A **harpy** is part woman, part vulture. What is another meaning of the word *harpy*? _____
_____
7. In mythology, each **dryad** lived in or near her own tree. What happened if someone cut down her tree? _____
8. In mythology, a **naiad** was a water nymph. Naiad is also the name of a moon orbiting which planet? _____
9. The word *naiad* also refers to the young of what insect? _____
10. If you could meet any mythological creature, what kind would it be? _____
Explain why you would like to meet it. _____
_____

ACTIVITY 155   Use Words in Context/   Name: _____

Describe a Fantasy Experience

Date: _____

Write a journal entry about a day spent in "Mythland." Describe the creatures you meet and what happens. Use at least six words from the list. Continue on another sheet of paper if you need more room to write.

basilisk	centaur	chimera	dryad	harpy	mermaid
minotaur	naiad	phoenix	satyr	sphinx	

_____

_____

_____

_____

_____

_____

_____

_____

_____

ACTIVITY 156   Test-Taking   Name: _____

Date: _____

Write the letter of the answer that best defines each mythological creature.

1. _____ basilisk
2. _____ centaur
3. _____ chimera
4. _____ dryad
5. _____ sphinx
6. _____ harpy
7. _____ mermaid
8. _____ minotaur
9. _____ naiad
10. _____ phoenix
11. _____ satyr

a. a creature with the head and upper body of a woman and wings and lower body of a vulture

b. a bird that lived for 500 years, then burst into flames and was reborn from the ashes

c. a fire-breathing creature that was part lion, goat, and serpent

d. a reptilian creature that turned people to stone with a glance

e. a creature with the head and upper body of a woman and the lower body of a lion

f. a water nymph

g. a creature with the upper part of a woman and lower part of a fish

h. a creature with the head and arms of a human and body of a horse

i. a creature with the upper body of a man and lower body of a goat

j. a creature with the body of a man and the head of a bull

k. a tree nymph

ACTIVITY 157 Define Heteronyms

Name: _____

Date: _____

Heteronyms are words that are spelled the same but have different pronunciations and meanings.   *Example:* He will not desert you in the desert.

All the words used below in italics are heteronyms. Use another sheet of paper to write your sentences. Use a dictionary if you need help with your answers.

1. When the accent is on the first syllable, *conduct* is a noun. It means behavior or how someone acts. Use *conduct* in a sentence as a noun.

2. When the accent is on the second syllable, *conduct* is a verb. It means to lead. Use *conduct* in a sentence as a verb.

3. When *record* is used as a noun, the accent is on the first syllable. Write a definition of *record* as a noun.

4. To *record* means to preserve in writing or in another form. When *record* is used this way, is it a noun or a verb? Which syllable has the accent?

5. When *produce* is used as a noun, what does it mean? Which syllable has the accent?

6. To *produce* means to make. The accent is on the second syllable. Write a sentence using *produce* as a verb.

ACTIVITY 158 Define Heteronyms

Name: _____

Date: _____

Use a dictionary if you need help with your answers.

1. To *present* means to give someone something. (The coach will <u>present</u> the award.) Which syllable is accented when *present* is used as a verb? _____

2. Another meaning of *present* is to be in a place at a given time. (I was <u>present</u> when the storm hit.) Which syllable is accented when *present* is used this way? _____

3. Is *present* a noun or a verb in this sentence? I have a <u>present</u> for you. _____ What does *present* mean as a noun? _____ Which syllable is accented? _____

4. *Present* can also be used as an adjective meaning current. (At the <u>present</u> time, we do not need any more purple balloons.) Which syllable is accented? _____

5. When *contest* is used as a noun, the accent is on the first syllable. What does *contest* mean in this sentence? Angelo won the <u>contest</u> because he guessed how many jelly beans were in the jar. _____

6. To *contest* means to argue or dispute a result. (If you believe there has been a mistake, you can <u>contest</u> the results.) Which syllable is accented? _____

7. What does the verb *project* mean? _____
Which syllable is accented? _____

8. Use *project* as a noun in a sentence. _____
_____

ACTIVITY 159 Define Heteronyms

Name: _____

Date: _____

| **Nouns:** | reb′ / el | re / quest′ | com′ / bine | ob′ / ject | prog′ / ress |
| **Verbs:** | re / bel′ | re′ / quest | com / bine′ | ob / ject′ | pro / gress′ |

1. A **rebel** is one who _____

2. To **rebel** means to _____

3. A **request** is _____

4. To **request** means to _____

5. A **combine** is a _____

6. To **combine** means to _____

7. An **object** is a _____

8. To **object** means to _____

9. **Progress** means _____

10. To **progress** means to _____

ACTIVITY 160 Determine Usage of Heteronyms

Name: _____

Date: _____

Write "N" for noun or "V" for verb to show how the boldface word in each sentence is used.

1. _____ A movie made in 1955 was titled **Rebel** *Without a Cause.*

2. _____ Would you **request** a copy of that movie from the library for me?

3. _____ When he lost the election, Dick wanted to **contest** the results.

4. _____ If everyone understands so far, we can **progress** to the next step.

5. _____ Marshall beat the **record** for the most hot peppers eaten in one minute.

6. _____ Would you **object** to wearing pink ribbons in your hair?

7. _____ At the toy factory, they **produce** 90 wagons a day.

8. _____ My **request** for a larger allowance was turned down.

9. _____ If you win the **contest**, you will get a free trip to Mount Fuji.

10. _____ Jana drove the **combine** at harvest time.

11. _____ Will you **conduct** the band today?

12. _____ Can you guess what **object** I have in this bag?

13. _____ Will someone **record** the results of the vote?

14. _____ Everyone should bring a **present** to the party.

15. _____ What type of **produce** should I pick up at the farmers' market?

ACTIVITY 161 Use Words in Context/ Write Question Sentences

Name:_____

Date:_____

Write a question sentence for each word. Write "N" for noun or "V" for verb on the line before the sentence to show how you used the word.

1. _____ combine _____

2. _____ conduct _____

3. _____ contest _____

4. _____ object _____

5. _____ present _____

6. _____ produce _____

7. _____ progress _____

8. _____ rebel _____

9. _____ record _____

10. _____ request _____

ACTIVITY 162 Test-Taking

Name:_____

Date:_____

Look at the accent mark. Pronounce the word out loud. Write "V" if the word is a verb or "N" if it is noun.

1. _____ rec' / ord

2. _____ pro / duce'

3. _____ pre / sent'

4. _____ reb' / el

5. _____ con' / test

6. _____ prog' / ress

7. _____ com' / bine

8. _____ pro' / duce

9. _____ con / duct'

10. _____ con / test'

11. _____ re / cord'

12. _____ pro / gress'

13. _____ re' / quest

14. _____ ob / ject'

15. _____ con' / duct

16. _____ ob' / ject

17. _____ com / bine'

18. _____ pres' / ent

19. _____ re / quest'

20. _____ re / bel'

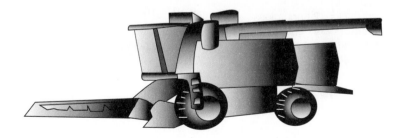

Answer Keys

Activity 1 (p. 1)
1. attorney   2. personnel
3. culprit   4. comrade
5. population   6. architect
7. ancestor   8. realtor
9. client   10. descendant
11. miser   12. peasants

Activity 2 (p. 1)
1. Personnel   2. attorney
3. miser   4. descendants
5. peasants   6. culprit
7. clients   8. comrades
9. population   10. ancestors
11. architect   12. realtor

Activity 3 (p. 2)
Answers will vary.

Activity 4 (p. 2)
1. F   2. F   3. F   4. F
5. F   6. T   7. T   8. F
9. T   10. F   11. T   12. F

Activity 5 (p. 3)
1. i   2. g   3. b   4. j
5. f   6. c   7. a   8. d
9. e   10. h

Activity 6 (p. 3)
Sentences will vary. Check spelling of past tense.

Activity 7 (p. 4)
1. barter   2. volleyed
3. mutter   4. attained
5. declined   6. quench
7. testified   8. trembled
9. minced   10. redeem

Activity 8 (p. 4)
1. b   2. a   3. a   4. d
5. c   6. b   7. c   8. d
9. b

Activity 9 (p. 5)
1. band/wagon   2. clock/wise
3. counterclock/wise 4. dead/line
5. fore/word   6. four/score
7. grand/stand   8. green/horn
9. hour/glass   10. steeple/jack
Definitions will vary. Check for reasonableness.

Activity 10 (p. 5)
1. Steeplejacks 2. hourglass
3. foreword   4. counterclockwise
5. grandstand   6. deadline
7. Fourscore   8. greenhorn
9. bandwagon

Activity 11 (p. 6)
Opinions will vary.

Activity 12 (p. 6)
1. F   2. F   3. F   4. F
5. F   6. T   7. T   8. F
9. F   10. T

Activity 13 (p. 7)
1. aloof   2. familiar
3. luxurious   4. jagged
5. dense   6. grateful
7. dreadful   8. absurd
9. gracious   10. energetic
11. frail

Activity 14 (p. 7)
Answers will vary. Check for reasonableness.

Activity 15 (p. 8)
1. dreadful   2. energetic
3. frail   4. dense
5. familiar   6. jagge
7. aloof   8. gratef
9. gracious   10. treme

Activity 16 (p. 8)
1. S   2. S   3. A
5. S   6. S   7. A
9. A   10. A   11. A   1
13. S   14. S   15. A   1
17. S   18. A   19. A   2
21. S   22. A   23. A   2

Activity 17 (p. 9)
1. aisle   2. prey
4. profit   5. duel
7. aid   8. alter
10. plain   11. bridle   1
13. plane   14. poor   1
16. hoard   17. pour   1

Activity 18 (p. 9)
1. hoard   2. bridle; sight
3. cite; site   4. prey
5. serial   6. aide
7. bridal; aisle; altar 8. duel
9. poor; pour
10. prophet; profit   11. cereal

Activity 19 (p. 10)
Answers will vary.

Activity 20 (p. 10)
1. a   2. d   3. a   4. c
5. d   6. a   7. b   8. b
9. d   10. b   11. c   12. d
13. a   14. b   15. c   16. b

Activity 21–22 (p. 11)
Answers will vary. Check for reasonableness.

Activity 23 (p. 12)
1. influence   2. schedule
3. secure   4. estimate
5. challenge   6. compromise
7. display   8. associate
9. experiments 10. patients

Activity 24 (p. 12)
1. b   2. c   3. b   4. a
5. c   6. c   7. d   8. a
9. b   10. c

Activity 25 (p. 13)
1. l   2. i   3. a   4. c
5. e   6. k   7. o   8. d
9. j   10. f   11. m   12. h
13. n   14. g   15. b

Activity 30–31 (p. 15–16)
Answers will vary.

Activity 32 (p. 16)
1. T   2. F   3. F   4. F
5. F   6. F   7. F   8. F
9. T   10. T   11. F   12. F

Activity 33 (p. 17)
1. defy   2. exceed
3. ignite   4. extinguish
5. contradict   6. slouch
7. dwindle   8. startle
9. unify   10. triumph

Activity 34 (p. 17)
1. unify   2. triumph
3. defy   4. ignite
5. postpone   6. extinguish
7. exceed   8. startled
9. dwindled   10. acquire
11. slouched   12. contradicted

Activity 35 (p. 18)
Answers will vary.

Activity 36 (p. 18)
1. c   2. d   3. b   4. b
5. a   6. d   7. c   8. c
9. a   10. b   11. c   12. d

Activity 37 (p. 19)
Answers will vary. Check for reasonableness.

Activity 38 (p. 19)
Answers will vary.

Activity 39 (p. 20)
1. petty   2. nutritious
3. significant   4. sufficient
5. frantic   6. scrawny
7. magnificent   8. versatile
9. spacious

Activity 40 (p. 20)
1. T   2. F   3. T   4. F
5. F   6. F   7. T   8. F
9. F   10. T   11. F   12. F

Activity 41 (p. 21)
1. draw / back   2. lay / away
3. view / point   4. gum / shoe
5. rip / cord   6. show / down
7. side / swipe   8. spend / thrift
9. trend / setter 10. turn / coat
Definitions will vary. Check for reasonableness.

Activity 42 (p. 21)
Answers will vary.

Activity 43 (p. 22)
Compound words will vary.

Activity 44 (p. 22)
1. T   2. F   3. F   4. T
5. T   6. F   7. T   8. F
9. T   10. F

Activity 45 (p. 23)
1. debate   2. issue
3. complex   4. issue
5. coast   6. debate
7. dice   8. issue
9. coast   10. dice

Activity 46 (p. 23)
1. draft   2. digest
3. commercial 4. exhaust
5. draft   6. commercial
7. focus   8. digest
9. focus   10. draft
11. exhaust   12. digest

Activity 47 (p. 24)
Answers will vary.

Activity 48 (p. 24)
1. g   2. f   3. d   4. j
5. c   6. h   7. e   8. b
9. a   10. i   11. f   12. e
13. i   14. a   15. j

Activity 49 (p. 25)
1. f   2. j   3. g   4. h
5. k   6. e   7. i   8. a
9. l   10. b   11. c   12. d
13. chose
14. assent/ascent; break/brake
15. advise; assent; brake; break;
    choose; chose; devise; loose; lose

Activity 50 (p. 25)
1. break   2. ascent; assent
3. loose; lose   4. devise
5. brake   6. advice; device
7. advise   8. choose
9. chose

Activity 51 (p. 26)
Answers will vary.

Activity 52 (p. 26)
1. T   2. F   3. T   4. T
5. T   6. T   7. T   8. F
9. T   10. F   11. F   12. T

Activity 53 (p. 27)
1. g   2. i   3. j   4. d
5. o   6. a   7. b   8. e
9. h   10. n   11. k   12. f
13. m   14. l   15. c

Activity 54 (p. 27)
1. d   2. o   3. m   4. e
5. b   6. n   7. c   8. a
9. f   10. l   11. i   12. g
13. k   14. h   15. j

Activity 55 (p. 28)
1. k   2. d   3. g   4. e
5. l   6. j   7. m   8. i
9. h   10. f   11. o   12. b
13. n   14. c   15. a

Activity 56 (p. 28)
1. f   2. l   3. g   4. h
5. i   6. e   7. k   8. a
9. d   10. b   11. c   12. n
13. o   14. j   15. m

Activity 57 (p. 29)
1. barrier   2. mural
3. pulley   4. parasites
5. capsule   6. infomercial
7. pesticides   8. textiles
9. accessories 10. brunch

Activity 58 (p. 29)
1. off the northern coast of Australia
2. The eggs of birds who ate insects poisoned with DDT were too thin. Fewer chicks hatched.
3. Answers will vary.
4. A capsule can be a small vehicle for astronauts.
5.–12. Answers will vary.

Activity 59 (p. 30)
1. accessory
2. to add items to match clothing worn
3. breakfast and lunch
4. information and commercial
5. usually gelatin
6. Pesticide is poisonous.
7.–10. Answers will vary.

Activity 60 (p. 30)
1. d   2. c   3. d   4. c
5. c   6. a   7. d   8. c
9. c   10. b

Activity 61 (p. 31)
Answers will vary. Check for reasonableness.

Activity 62 (p. 31)
1. achievement 2. nourishment
3. commandment   4. achieve
5. enrollment
6. command (or commandment)
7. requires   8. enroll
9. harasses   10. requirements

Activity 63 (p. 32)
1. O   2. O   3. O   4. O
5. F   6. O   7. F   8. O
9. F   10. F   11. F   12. F

Activity 64 (p. 32)
1. c   2. b   3. b   4. d
5. a   6. c   7. b   8. a
9. b   10. d

Activity 65 (p. 33)
1. high-/handed   2. stout/hearted
3. open/handed   4. under/handed
5. free/hand   6. long/hand
7. short/handed   8. short/hand
9. fore/hand

Activity 66 (p. 33)
Answers will vary. Some possible words are: barehanded; beforehand; cowhand; evenhanded; farmhand; handball; handcrafted; handcuffs; handgrip; handrail; handset; handshake; handwritten; offhand; secondhand; stagehand

Activity 67 (p. 34)
1. longhand   2. shorthand
3. high-handed   4. underhanded
5. openhanded   6. freehand
7. stouthearted 8. shorthanded
9. forehand   10. thumbtack

Activity 68 (p. 34)
1. F   2. T   3. F   4. F
5. T   6. T   7. F   8. F
9. F   10. T

Activity 69 (p. 35)
1. capable   2. hasty
3. indifferent   4. defiant
5. meek   6. unbearable
7. hostile   8. hesitant
9. jubilant   10. deliberate

Activity 70 (p. 35)
Answers will vary.

Activity 71 (p. 36)
Journal entries will vary.

Activity 72 (p. 36)
1. A   2. S   3. S   4. S
5. S   6. A   7. S   8. A
9. S   10. S   11. A   12. A
13. A   14. A   15. S   16. S
17. A   18. A   19. A   20. S

Activity 73–74 (p. 37)
Answers will vary. Check for
reasonableness.

Activity 75 (p. 38)
1. V   2. V   3. V   4. N
5. N   6. A   7. N   8. N
9. V   10. A   11. N

Activity 76 (p. 38)
1. N   2. V   3. V   4. V
5. N   6. V   7. N   8. N
9. V   10. N   11. N   12. A

Activity 77 (p. 39)
1. i   2. f   3. j   4. a
5. h   6. d   7. c   8. g
9. e   10. b

Activity 78 (p. 39)
Sentences will vary.
1. disadvantage   2. inappropriate
3. incompetent   4. unconscious
5. unfamiliar   6. informal
7. illegible   8. impractical
9. dissatisfied   10. intolerable

Activity 79 (p. 40)
1. informal
2. appropriate; inappropriate; formal
3. advantage

4. disadvantage; unfamiliar
5. illegible; legible
6. practical; impractical
7. conscious; intolerable
8. tolerable

Activity 80 (p. 40)
1. b   2. b   3. d   4. a
5. b   6. a   7. d   8. c
9. c   10. b   11. a   12. b

Activity 81 (p. 41)
1. h   2. j   3. l   4. n
5. b   6. c   7. k   8. g
9. e   10. i   11. a   12. d
13. o   14. f   15. m

Activity 82 (p. 41)
1. a   2. c   3. k   4. h
5. f   6. i   7. d   8. b
9. g   10. l   11. n   12. j
13. e   14. o   15. m

Activity 83 (p. 42)
1. n   2. h   3. e   4. d
5. l   6. g   7. c   8. k
9. b   10. m   11. o   12. i
13. a   14. f   15. j

Activity 84 (p. 42)
1. h   2. n   3. b   4. l
5. j   6. i   7. d   8. c
9. a   10. g   11. e   12. f
13. m   14. k   15. o

Activity 85 (p. 43)
1. dispenser   2. portrait
3. employer   4. hermit
5. salon   6. vendor
7. suburb   8. mansion
9. siblings   10. buffet
11. fugitive   12. spectator

Activity 86 (p. 43)
People: employer; fugitive; hermit;
siblings; spectator; vendor
Places: mansion; salon; suburb
Things: buffet; dispenser; portrait

Activity 87 (p. 44)
Headlines will vary.

Activity 88 (p. 44)
1. a   2. d   3. a   4. b
5. c   6. b   7. a   8. c

Activity 89 (p. 45)
1. fidget   2. convey
3. hover   4. simmer
5. condense   6. dilate
7. cater   8. emphasize
9. impound   10. shuffle
11. meander   12. meddle

Activity 90 (p. 45)
1. convey   2. emphasize
3. fidget   4. meander
5. simmer   6. meddle
7. shuffle   8. impound
9. hover   10. dilate

Activity 91 (p. 46)
Sentences will vary. Check for spelling
of past tense verbs.

Activity 92 (p. 46)
1. S   2. S   3. S   4. A
5. S   6. A   7. S   8. A
9. S   10. S   11. S   12. A
13. A   14. S   15. S   16. A
17. S   18. A   19. A   20. A
21. A   22. A

Activity 93 (p. 47)
1. entertain   2. amaze
3. encourage   4. enforce
5. enlarge   6. advance
7. equip   8. confine
9. retire   10. detach

Activity 94 (p. 47)
1. advancement   2. amazement
3. confinement   4. detachment
5. encouragement 6. enforcement
7. enlargement   8. entertainment
9. equipment   10. retirement
Definitions will vary.

Activity 95 (p. 48)
1. enlarge   2. entertainment
3. equipment   4. equip
5. advance   6. amazement
7. entertain   8. enlargement
9. retirement   10. advancement
11. retire   12. amaze

Activity 96 (p. 48)
1. A   2. S   3. S   4. A
5. S   6. A   7. S   8. S
9. A   10. S   11. A   12. A
13. A   14. S   15. S   16. A
17. A   18. S

Activity 97 (p. 49)
1. freelance   2. dragnet
3. standoff   4. gatecrasher
5. downtrodden   6. lukewarm
7. foresight   8. barnstorm
9. undermine   10. fortnight

Activity 98 (p. 49)
Answers will vary.

Activity 99 (p. 50)
News articles will vary.

Activity 100 (p. 50)
1. d   2. b   3. c   4. a
5. a   6. d   7. c   8. b
9. b

Activity 101 (p. 51)
1. reigns   2. board   3. straight
4. principle 5. peak   6. bored
7. pique   8. principal
9. stationery   10. reins
11. strait   12. stationary

Activity 102 (p. 51)
1. peek; peak   2. piqued; peek
3. principles   4. principals; Board
5. principal   6. bored; stationary
7. stationery   8. reigns; reins
9. straight; Strait

Activity 103 (p. 52)
Rhymes will vary.

Activity 104 (p. 52)
1. a   2. b   3. a   4. a
5. a   6. a   7. b   8. c
9. c   10. b   11. a   12. a
13. b   14. a   15. b

Activity 105 (p. 53)
1. e   2. c   3. f   4. a
5. d   6. g   7. h   8. b

Activity 106 (p. 53)
Definitions and sentences will vary.
Check for reasonableness.
Root words:
1. accumulate   2. cancel
3. comprehend   4. duplicate
5. extend   6. occupy
7. oppose   8. supervise

Activity 107 (p. 54)
Answers will vary.

Activity 108 (p. 54)
1. b   2. p   3. h   4. c
5. l   6. m   7. f   8. k
9. a   10. o   11. g   12. i
13. n   14. d   15. j   16. e

Activity 109 (p. 55)
1. h   2. c   3. g   4. o
5. j   6. e   7. m   8. b
9. a   10. l   11. d   12. i
13. k   14. f   15. n

Activity 110 (p. 55)
1. b   2. a   3. j   4. g
5. l   6. k   7. f   8. i
9. m   10. n   11. h   12. c
13. o   14. e   15. d

Activity 111 (p. 56)
1. k   2. j   3. o   4. n
5. a   6. l   7. g   8. f
9. d   10. i   11. e   12. m
13. b   14. h   15. c

Activity 112 (p. 56)
1. i   2. k   3. j   4. e
5. f   6. a   7. h   8. b
9. l   10. m   11. g   12. o
13. d   14. n   15. c

Activity 113 (p. 57)
1. h   2. c   3. g   4. a
5. i   6. d   7. f   8. j
9. b   10. e

Activity 114 (p. 57)
1. admiration   2. determination
3. evaluation   4. exaggeration
5. hesitation   6. negotiation
7. prohibition   8. provocation
9. reservation   10. substitution
Definitions may vary. Check for
reasonableness.

Activity 115 (p. 58)
Answers will vary.

Activity 116 (p. 58)
1. F   2. F   3. F   4. T
5. T   6. T   7. T   8. F
9. T   10. T   11. T   12. F
13. F   14. T   15. T

Activity 117 (p. 59)
1. affect   2. continual
3. irritate   4. continuous
5. aggravate   6. altogether
7. effect   8. accept
9. all together   10. brought
11. bought   12. except

Activity 118 (p. 59)
1. all together   2. irritated
3. except   4. altogether
5. effect   6. brought; bought
7. accepted   8. aggravated
9. effect   10. continual
11. affected   12. continuous

Activity 119 (p. 60)
Questions will vary. Check that
sentences end in a question mark.

Activity 120 (p. 60)
1. b   2. a   3. b   4. a
5. a   6. c   7. c   8. d
9. d   10. c   11. b   12. b

Activity 121 (p. 61)
1. d   2. f   3. i   4. a
5. j   6. e   7. c   8. b
9. h   10. g

Activity 122 (p. 61)
1. gratuity   2. limitation
3. duration: epidemic
4. hazard   5. minority
6. majority   7. census
8. autobiography   9. biography
Answers to questions will vary.

Activity 123 (p. 62)
Definitions may vary.
1. limit   2. major
3. minor   4. writing
5. something biological that is
   dangerous
6. every 10 years
7.–8. Answers will vary.

Activity 124 (p. 62)
1. b   2. c   3. b   4. d
5. a   6. b   7. a   8. c

Activity 125 (p. 63)
Answers will vary. Check for
reasonableness.

Activity 126 (p. 63)
1. detective; considerable
2. detector; reconsider
3. cooperation; alternate
4. consideration; alternative
5. alteration; undetectable
6. inconsiderate; cooperative

Activity 127 (p. 64)
Answers will vary.

Activity 128 (p. 64)
1. c   2. c   3. d   4. a
5. b   6. c   7. a   8. b

Activity 129 (p. 65)
1. canopy   2. bouillon
3. residence   4. canapé
5. peddle   6. compliment
7. humorous   8. pedal
9. residents   10. humerus
11. bullion   12. complement

Activity 130 (p. 65)
1. Bullion   2. peddlers
3. canopy   4. pedal; humerus
5. residents; residence; canapés
6. complimented; bouillon
7. complemented
8. humorous   9. pedaled

Activity 131 (p. 66)
Answers will vary.

Activity 132 (p. 66)
1. b   2. a   3. b   4. b
5. b   6. a   7. a   8. b
9. a   10. b   11. b   12. a
13. a

Activity 133 (p. 67)
1. flag/stone
2. mile/stone
3. earth/work
4. light-/headed
5. fan/fare
6. keep/sake
7. hay/wire
8. work/horse
9. carry/over
10. fore/ground
11. safe/guard
12. pussy/foot

Activity 134 (p. 67)
1. light-headed
2. keepsake
3. foreground
4. carryover
5. pussyfoot
6. workhorse
7. milestone
8. earthworks
9. safeguards

Activity 135 (p. 68)
Answers will vary.

Activity 136 (p. 68)
1. h
2. k
3. l
4. b
5. d
6. f
7. g
8. j
9. a
10. e
11. c
12. i

Activity 137 (p. 69)
1. e
2. k
3. n
4. h
5. a
6. i
7. d
8. j
9. m
10. l
11. o
12. c
13. b
14. g
15. f

Activity 138 (p. 69)
1. a
2. j
3. l
4. m
5. c
6. d
7. f
8. g
9. h
10. k
11. b
12. o
13. n
14. e
15. i

Activity 139 (p. 70)
1. n
2. a
3. m
4. f
5. i
6. j
7. e
8. o
9. k
10. h
11. l
12. c
13. g
14. d
15. b

Activity 140 (p. 70)
1. k
2. a
3. i
4. m
5. n
6. l
7. j
8. d
9. e
10. h
11. g
12. c
13. o
14. f
15. b

Activity 141 (p. 71)
Answers will vary. Check for reasonableness.

Activity 142 (p. 71)
1. directly; director; observatory; investigator
2. observant; directory
3. investors; proposed; investigate
4. proposal; investigation
5. direct; observation

Activity 143 (p. 72)
1. V
2. N
3. N
4. V
5. N
6. N
7. N
8. N
9. V
10. V
11. N
12. N
13. V
14. N
15. N
16. N
17. V
18. N
19. N

Activity 144 (p. 72)
1. T
2. F
3. T
4. F
5. F
6. T
7. T
8. F
9. F
10. T
11. T
12. F
13. T
14. T
15. F
16. T

Activity 145 (p. 73)
1. table/land
2. dough/boy
3. jitter/bug
4. lady/finger
5. over/sight
6. sand/hog
7. under/coat
8. high/brow
9. under/tow
10. flag/ship

Activity 146 (p. 73)
Answers may vary.

Activity 147 (p. 74)
Headlines will vary.

Activity 148 (p. 74)
1. F
2. F
3. F
4. T
5. T
6. F
7. F
8. T
9. F
10. F
11. T
12. F
13. T
14. T
15. F
16. F
17. F

Activity 149 (p. 75)
1. 4 children born at the same time
2. 4; 5
3. 8
4. 3
5. 5
6. 1
7. 10
8. 2
9. 10
10. 100
11. 1,000
12. every 200 years
13. every 150 years

Activity 150–151 (p. 75–76)
Answers will vary.

Activity 152 (p. 76)
1. c
2. b
3. b
4. c
5. d
6. b
7. a
8. b
9. a
10. c

Activity 153 (p. 77)
1. phoenix
2. sphinx
3. centaur
4. satyr
5. harpy
6. mermaid
7. chimera
8. basilisk
9. dryad
10. naiad
11. minotaur

Activity 154 (p. 77)
1. Phoenix
2. Minos
3. It was a huge maze.
4. Theseus
5. Giza, Egypt
6. A nagging, unpleasant woman
7. The dryad died.
8. Jupiter
9. dragonfly
10. Answers will vary.

Activity 155 (p. 78)
Journal entries will vary.

Activity 156 (p. 78)
1. d
2. h
3. c
4. k
5. e
6. a
7. g
8. j
9. f
10. b
11. i

Activity 157 (p. 79)
1.–2. Answers will vary.
3. a written account of an event
4. verb; second
5. fruits and vegetables; first
6. Answer will vary.

Activity 158 (p. 79)
1. second
2. first
3. noun; a gift; first
4. first
5. competition
6. second
7. to make louder or more visible; second
8. Answer will vary.

Activity 159 (p. 80)
1. is rebellious or disobedient.
2. disobey someone in authority.
3. an instance of asking for something.
4. ask for something.
5. harvesting machine.
6. join or unite; to harvest a crop.
7. thing or item.
8. to oppose or argue against.
9. forward or onward movement.
10. move forward; to get better.

Activity 160 (p. 80)
1. N
2. V
3. V
4. V
5. N
6. V
7. V
8. N
9. N
10. N
11. V
12. N
13. V
14. N
15. N

Activity 161 (p. 81)
Sentences will vary. Check noun or verb answers.

Activity 162 (p. 81)
1. N
2. V
3. V
4. N
5. N
6. N
7. N
8. N
9. V
10. V
11. V
12. V
13. V
14. V
15. N
16. N
17. V
18. N
19. N
20. V